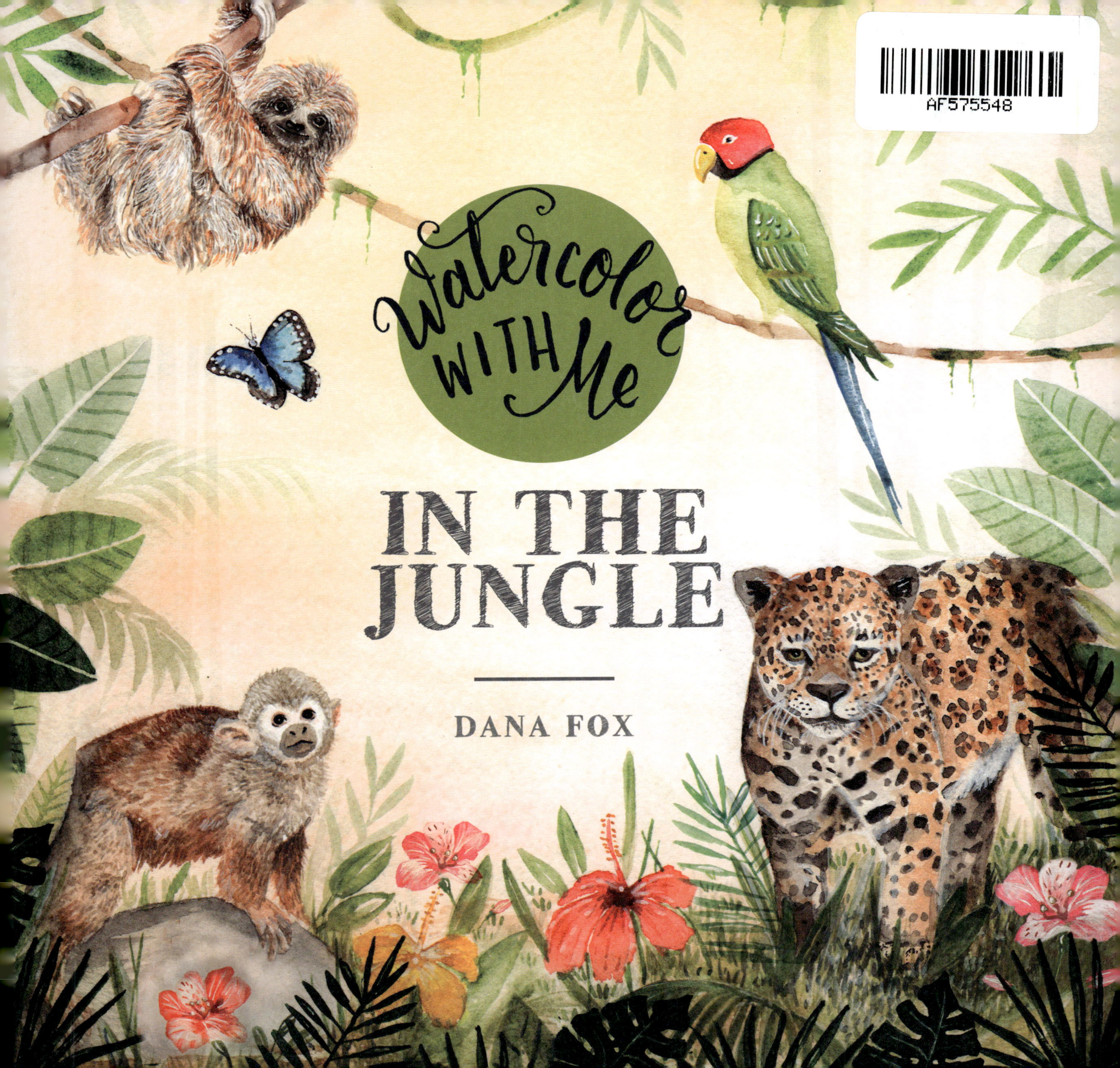
Watercolor
WITH Me
IN THE
JUNGLE
DANA FOX

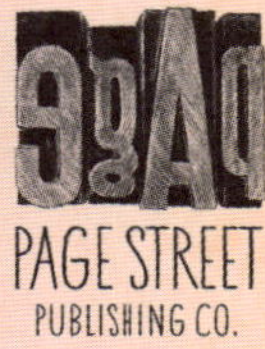

First published in 2020 by
Page Street Publishing Co.
27 Congress Street, Suite 1511
Salem, MA 01970
www.pagestreetpublishing.com

Distributed by Macmillan, sales in Canada by The Canadian Manda Group.

28 27 26 25 5 6 7 8

ISBN-13: 978-1-64567-112-1
ISBN-10: 1-64567-112-7

Library of Congress Control Number: 2019957264

Cover and book design by Dana Fox
Illustrations by Dana Fox

Printed and bound in China

Page Street Publishing protects our planet by donating to nonprofits like The Trustees, which focuses on local land conservation.

TABLE OF CONTENTS

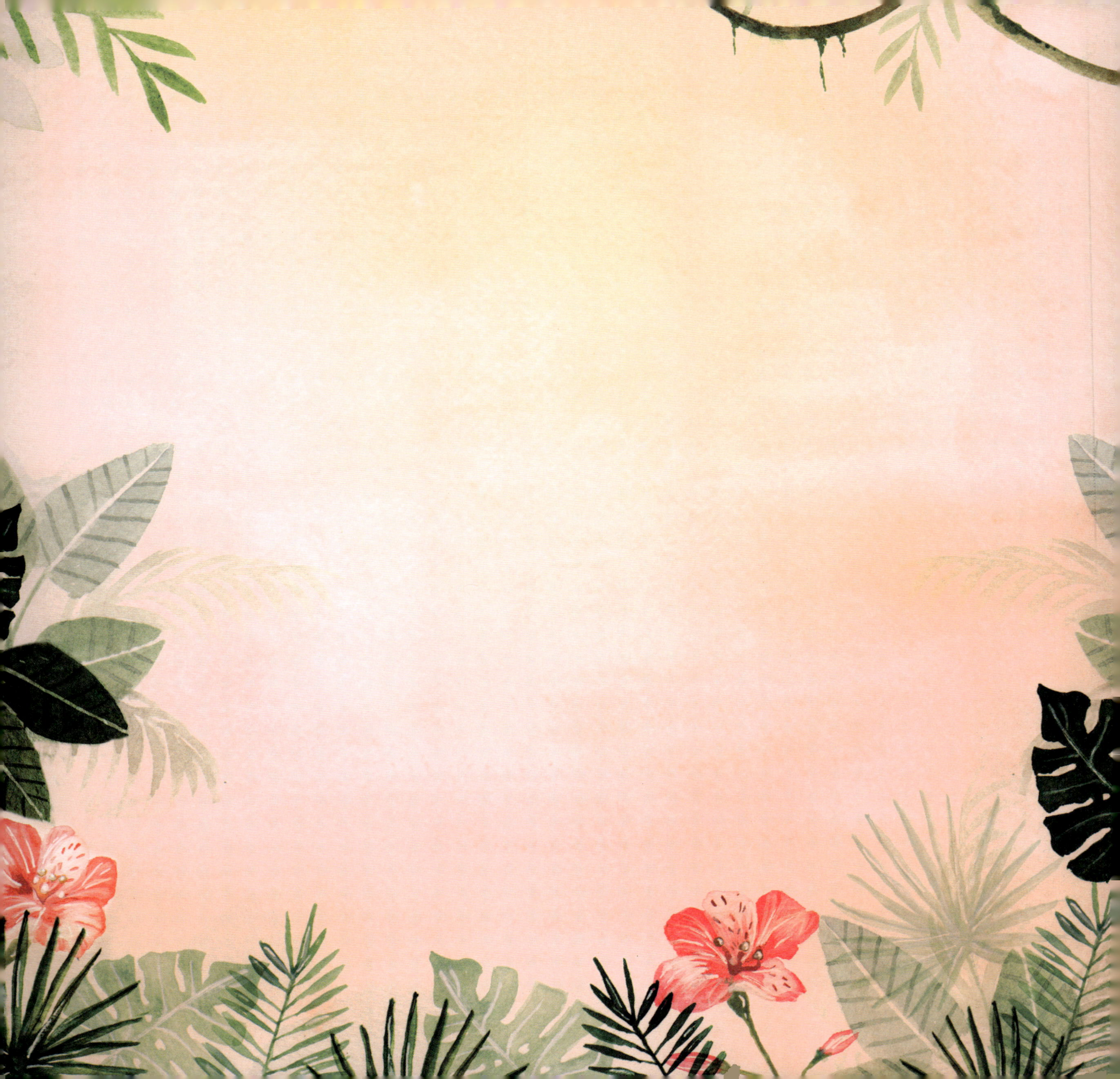

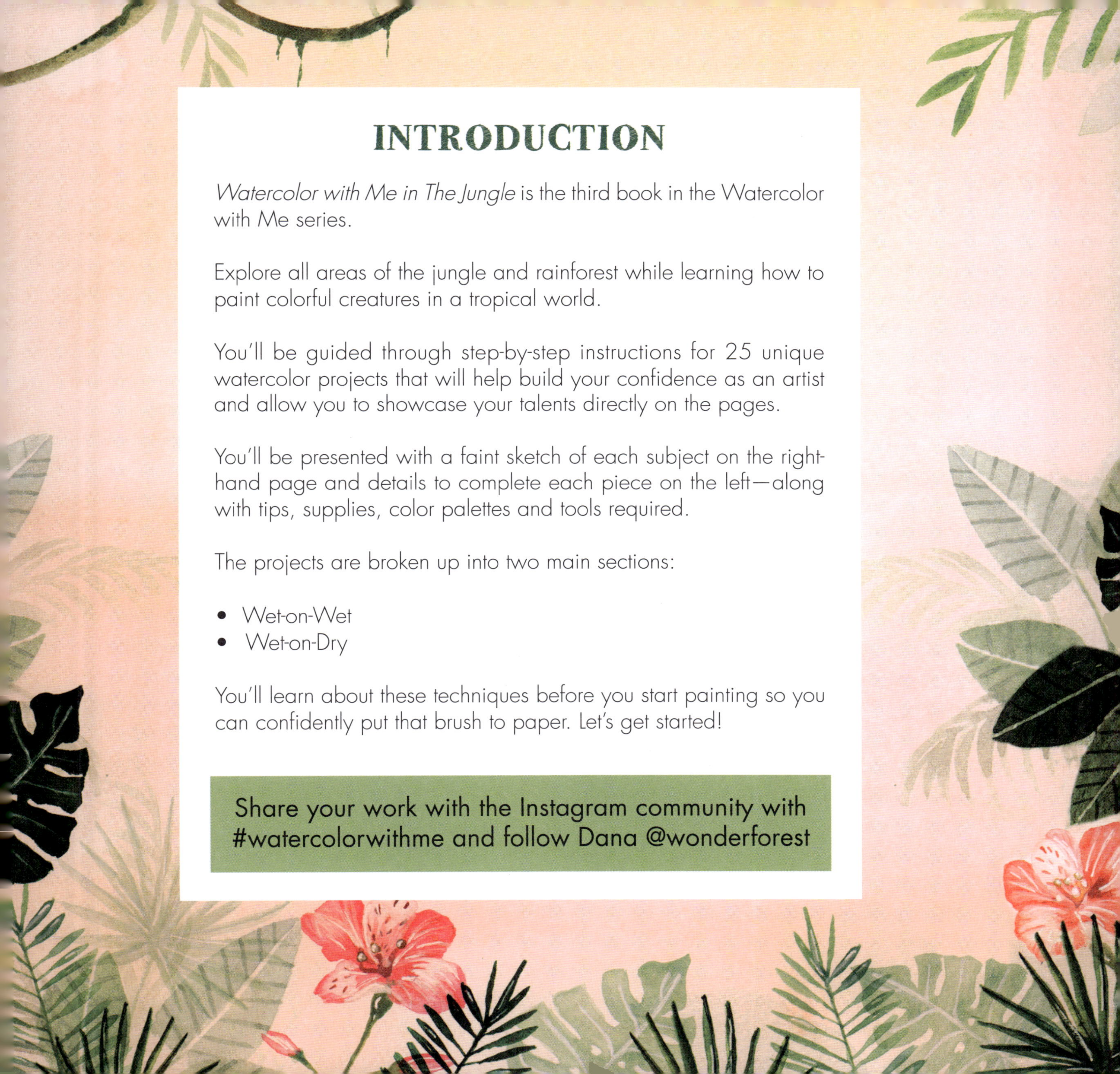

INTRODUCTION

Watercolor with Me in The Jungle is the third book in the Watercolor with Me series.

Explore all areas of the jungle and rainforest while learning how to paint colorful creatures in a tropical world.

You'll be guided through step-by-step instructions for 25 unique watercolor projects that will help build your confidence as an artist and allow you to showcase your talents directly on the pages.

You'll be presented with a faint sketch of each subject on the right-hand page and details to complete each piece on the left—along with tips, supplies, color palettes and tools required.

The projects are broken up into two main sections:

- Wet-on-Wet
- Wet-on-Dry

You'll learn about these techniques before you start painting so you can confidently put that brush to paper. Let's get started!

Share your work with the Instagram community with #watercolorwithme and follow Dana @wonderforest

MASTER COLOR CHART

All illustrations in this book use the Winsor & Newton Cotman line of watercolor paints for their affordability and quality. Below are the colors used in the projects for your color matching reference. Due to print matching and the amount of water used, actual paint hues may vary slightly from these samples.

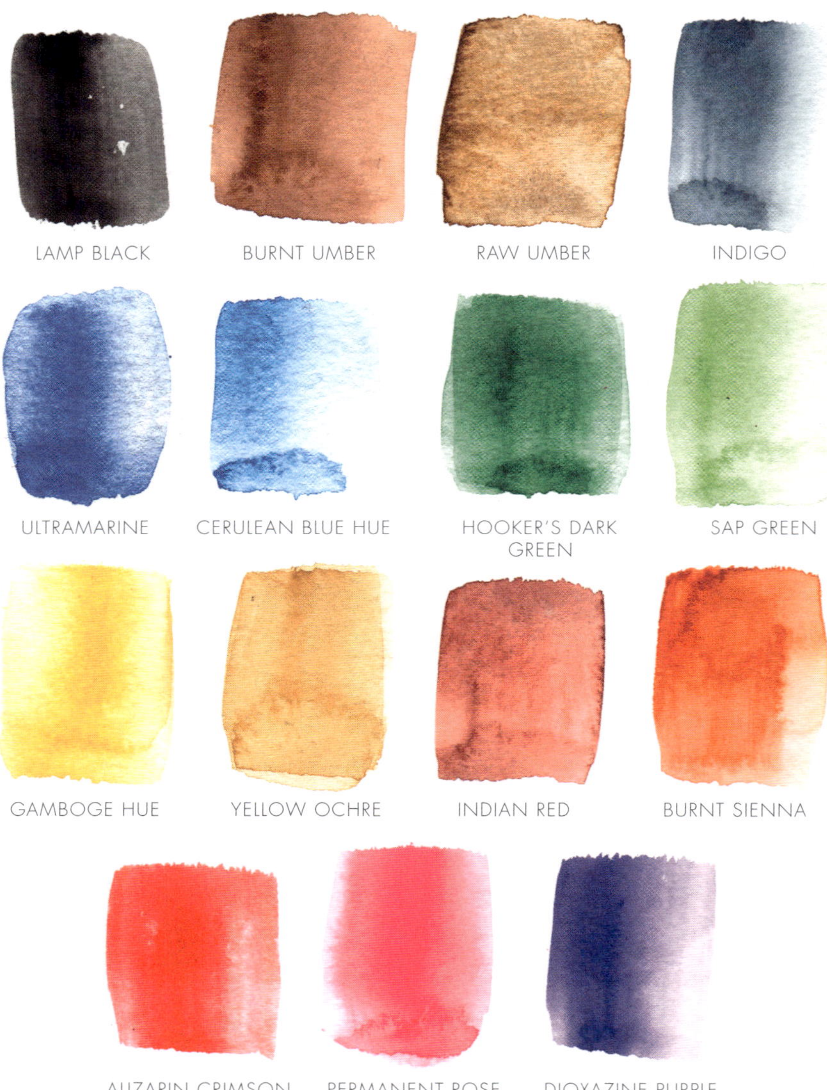

Supplies you'll likely need:

Watercolor paint
Clean water
Mixing palette
Round watercolor brushes (sizes 2–6)
Fine detail brush
Black permanent ink pen
White gel pen
Paper towels

GET YOUR SUPPLIES

To purchase the products used in this book, please visit my Amazon shop at: http://amazon.com/shop/wonderforest

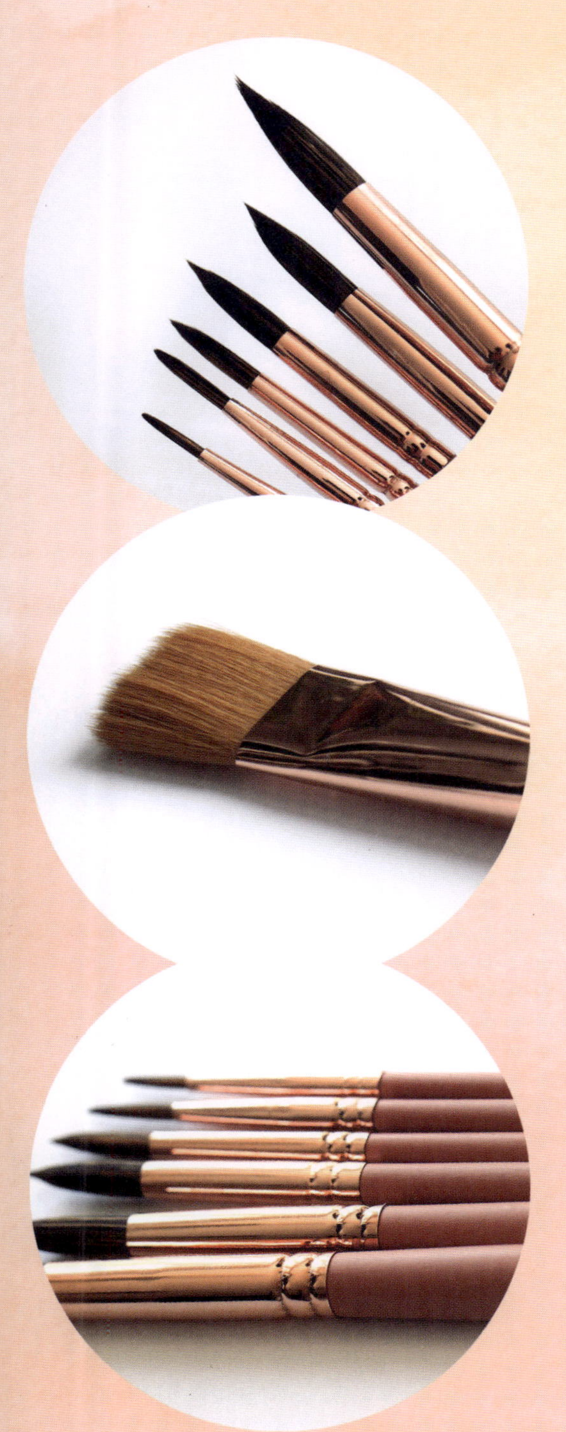

PAINTING WITH ANIMALS IN MIND

As a watercolor artist and animal lover, I ventured out to create a brush that not only performed well, but was made of premium 100 percent synthetic brush fibers.

I developed a line of cruelty-free watercolor brushes with bristles that are incredibly soft, absorbent and as flexible as genuine fur-based brushes.

A set of six round brushes includes sizes 2, 4, 6, 8, 10 and 12. The tips of the brushes are ultra pointed to razor precision for the finest detail work, no matter the size, and they snap back to a point without fraying!

The 1″ Wash Brush is perfect for filling larger areas and is made from the softest synthetic bristles you'll ever find.

These brushes make the perfect companion to this book.

You can purchase them on the official Wonder Forest online store at:

www.wonderforest.com

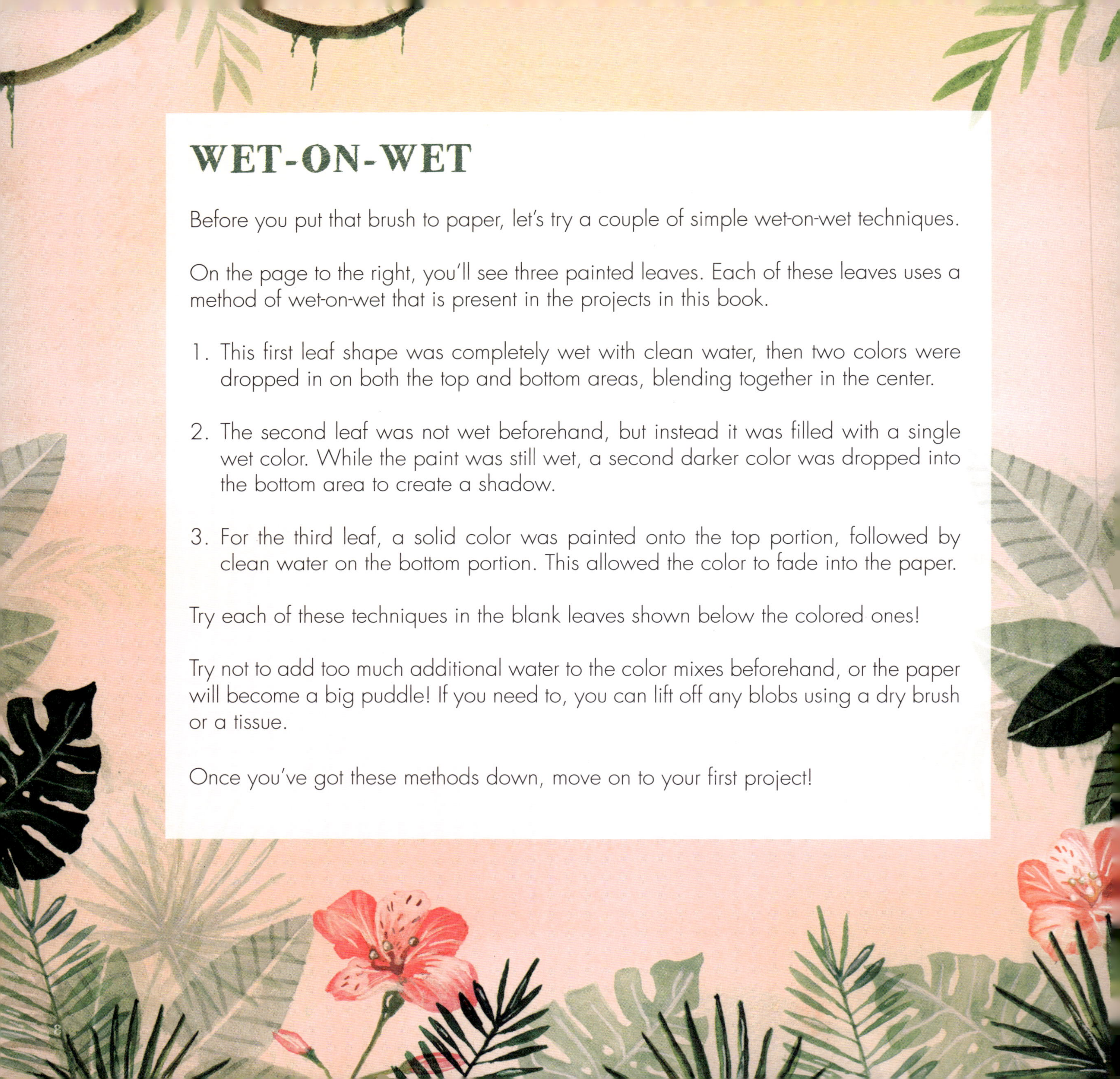

WET-ON-WET

Before you put that brush to paper, let's try a couple of simple wet-on-wet techniques.

On the page to the right, you'll see three painted leaves. Each of these leaves uses a method of wet-on-wet that is present in the projects in this book.

1. This first leaf shape was completely wet with clean water, then two colors were dropped in on both the top and bottom areas, blending together in the center.

2. The second leaf was not wet beforehand, but instead it was filled with a single wet color. While the paint was still wet, a second darker color was dropped into the bottom area to create a shadow.

3. For the third leaf, a solid color was painted onto the top portion, followed by clean water on the bottom portion. This allowed the color to fade into the paper.

Try each of these techniques in the blank leaves shown below the colored ones!

Try not to add too much additional water to the color mixes beforehand, or the paper will become a big puddle! If you need to, you can lift off any blobs using a dry brush or a tissue.

Once you've got these methods down, move on to your first project!

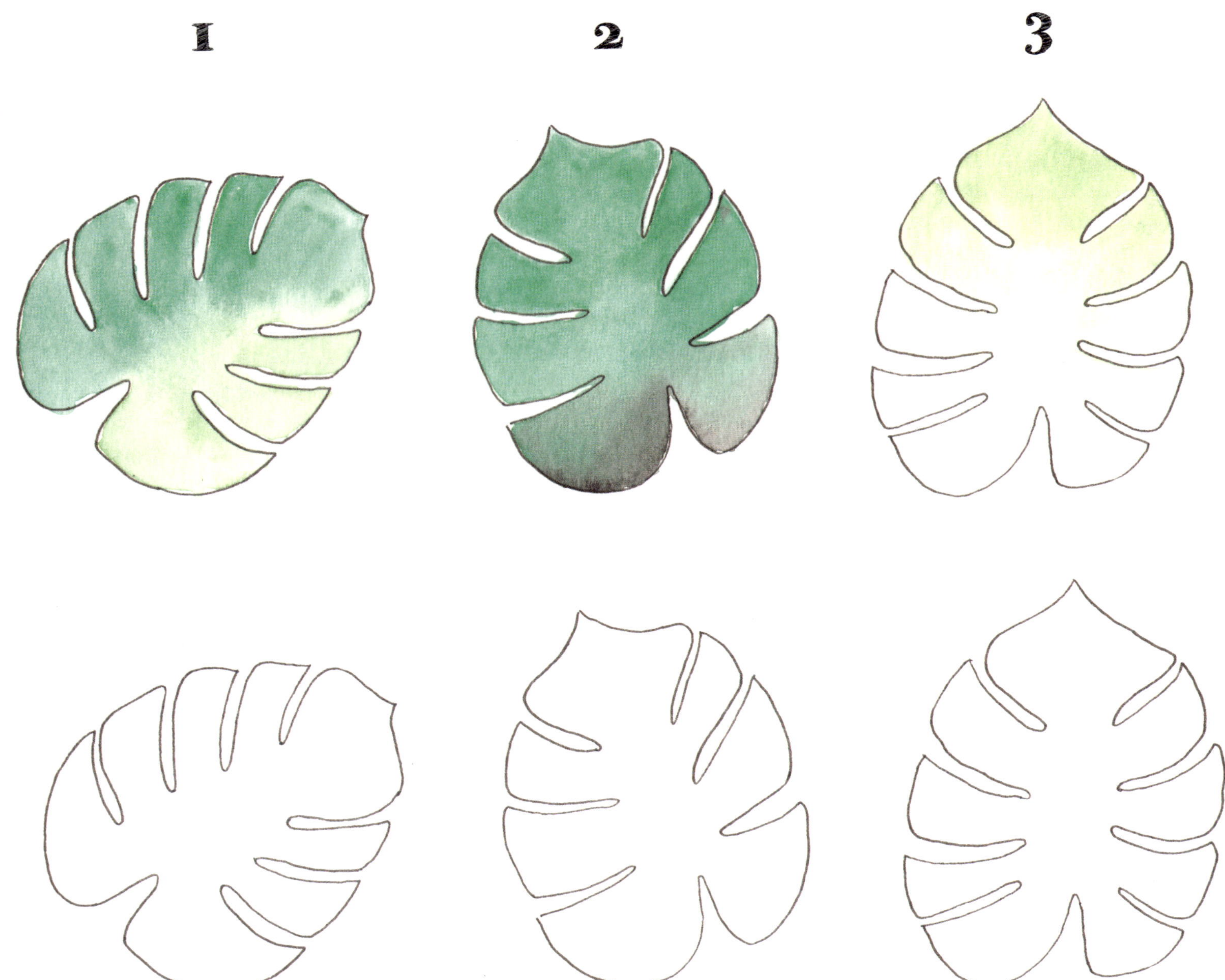
1
2
3

Hibiscus

The hibiscus is a tropical flower that comes in many color varieties. For this project, you'll experiment with blending two different colors in a wet area to create a pretty flower of your own!

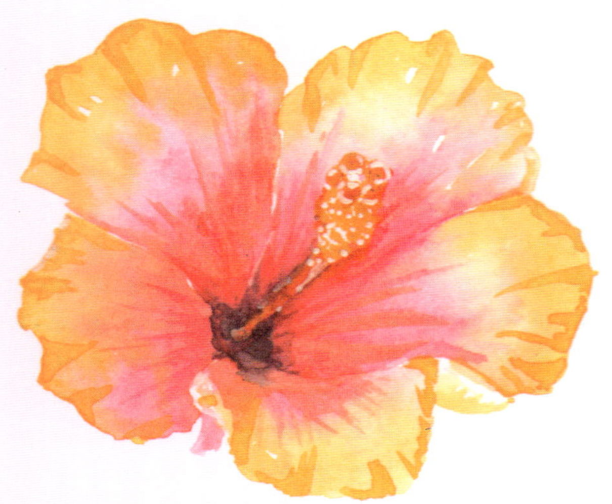

COLOR CHART

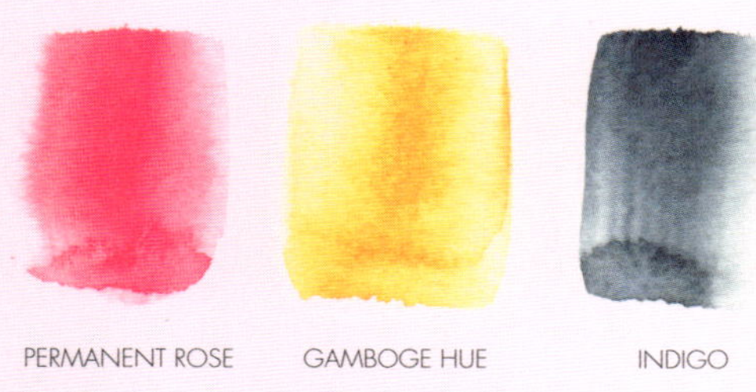

SUPPLIES

- Round brush (size 6 works well)
- Clean water
- 3 colors of paint
- White ink pen

1. Fill in one of the single petals using clean water only. While the paper is still damp, drop some Permanent Rose into the inside portion of the petal and allow it to blend toward the top.
2. While the paint is still wet, drop Gamboge Hue onto the top edge of the petal, using the tip of your brush to carefully shape the outside edge until it is crisp.
3. Wipe the color off your brush and use the tip to blend and coax the two colors together where they meet in the center.
4. Repeat this process for each petal, letting them dry before moving onto the next.
5. Paint the center stalk of the stamen with Permanent Rose and the top portion with Gamboge Hue. Let dry completely.
6. Using Indigo, paint the center of the flower and around the stamen to create a shadow effect.
7. With the flower dry, paint swift strokes of the same colors onto each petal. Finish by adding a few dots to the stamen tip with the white ink pen.

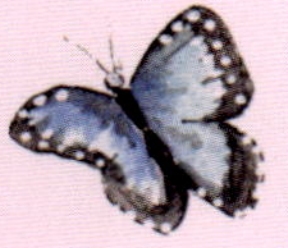

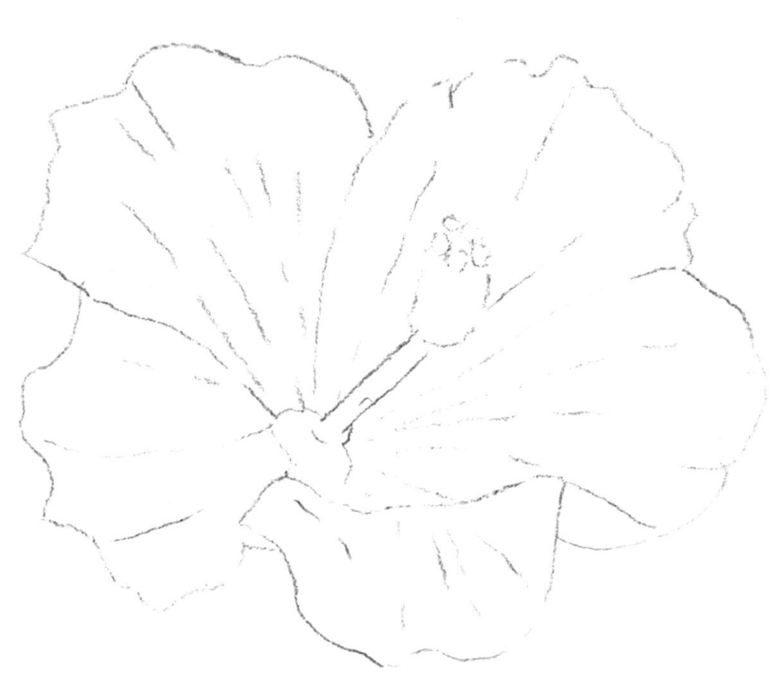

Blue Morpho Butterfly

The gorgeous bright blue tones in this butterfly allow it to really stand out and glisten in the sunlight. You'll create a wet-on-wet base of blues and add details using the tip of your brush.

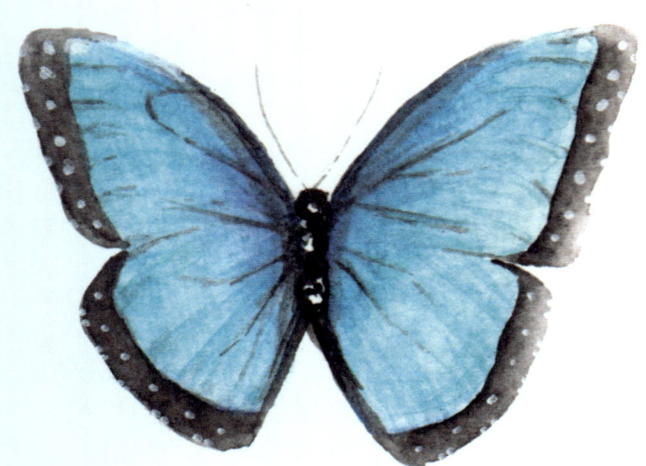

COLOR CHART

CERULEAN BLUE HUE

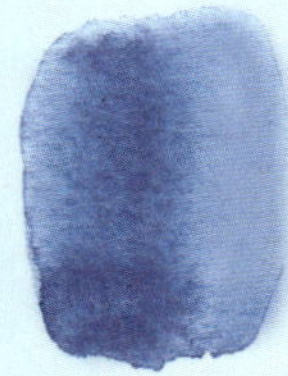

ULTRAMARINE

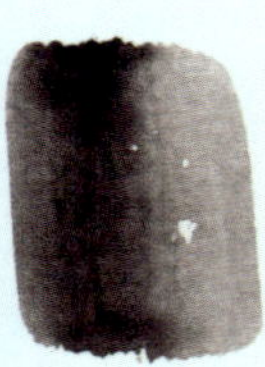

LAMP BLACK

SUPPLIES

- Round brush (size 6 works well)
- Clean water
- 3 colors of paint
- White ink pen

1. On dry paper, fill in both the left and right wings completely with a diluted mix of Cerulean Blue Hue. Before the paint dries, drop in some Ultramarine to the inside edges of the butterfly.
2. Let the paint dry completely. Using Lamp Black, paint the wing tips entirely and let them dry.
3. Using a diluted mixture of Cerulean Blue Hue, paint swift strokes onto the wings, starting from the inside edge and extending out towards the wing tips. This will add that streaky appearance and texture.
4. Once the paint is dry, fill in the center body of the butterfly with Lamp Black. Add the same color to the interior edges of the wings.
5. With the very tip of your brush, paint the detail lines onto the wings and add the antennae.
6. Using a white ink pen, add the dots to the wing tips and some highlights to the body of the butterfly.

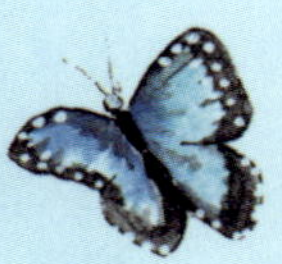

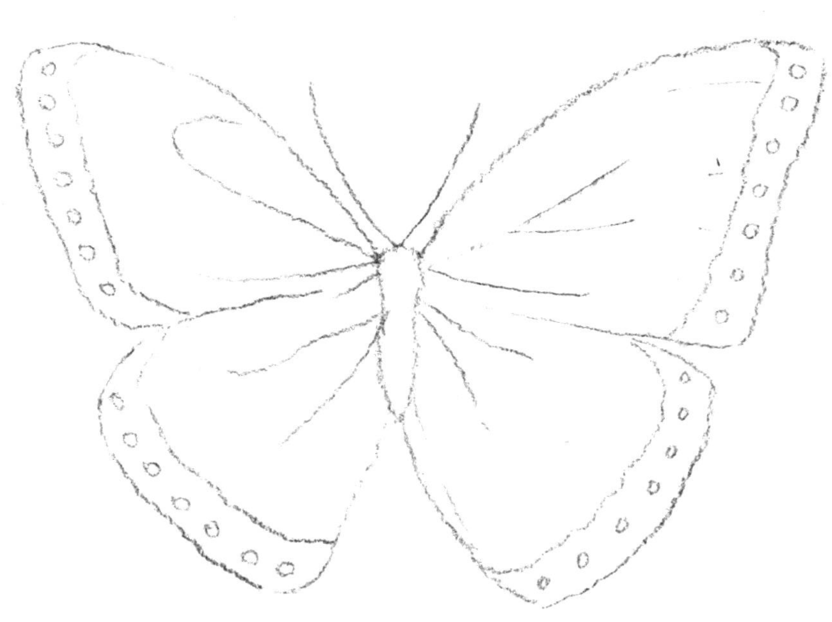

Black Panther

With his shiny black coat and slick appearance, this panther only requires one main color to come to life.

You'll create this painting by working on one section of the body at a time in a wet-on-wet fashion.

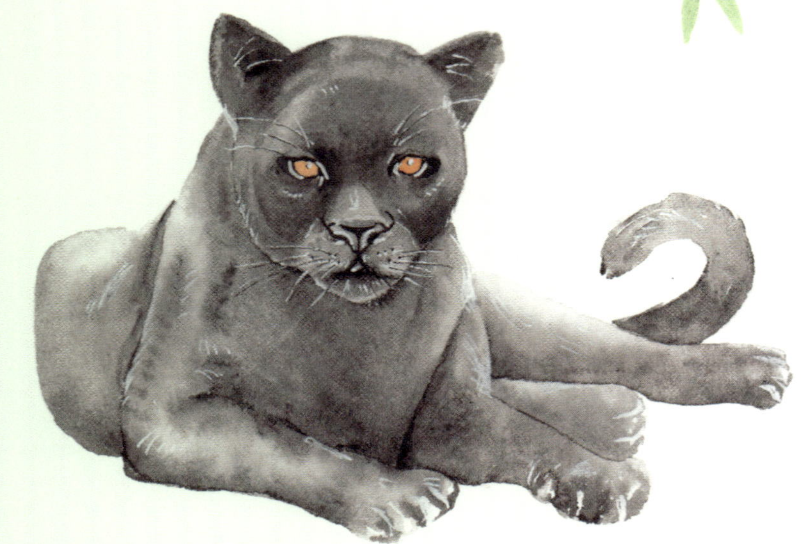

COLOR CHART

LAMP BLACK YELLOW OCHRE

SUPPLIES

- Round brush (size 6 works well)
- Clean water
- 2 colors of paint
- White ink pen
- Size 1 black ink pen

1. Starting on the left-hand section of the body, fill in the area completely with clean water. The paper should be damp.

2. Using a 50/50 mixture of Lamp Black and water, apply to the damp area. To create darker areas along the bottom edge and behind the front leg, drop in a more concentrated mix of the Lamp Black.

3. While this area dries, move on to the opposite side of the panther. Dampen the top of the back leg with water and once again apply your 50/50 mixture of paint to the bottom edge of the back leg, allowing the paint to gradually fade out near the top.

4. While that area dries, move on to the right-hand front leg and use the same technique, darkening any shadowed areas with a more pigmented mix of the Lamp Black.

5. Allow your work to dry and fill in the whole front chest and left-hand leg section with water. Using your same mixture, fill the area. Dry your brush off and use it to lift out any highlighted areas on the arm. Complete the remaining foot and tail in the same way.

6. Wet the head and apply your paint in accordance with the sample picture. Darker areas include the ears and around the eyes. Lighter areas include the nose and mouth area.

7. Once dry, add Yellow Ochre to the eyes. Let dry and use your white ink pen to add highlights and whiskers to the face as well as the toes. Use your black ink pen to define the nose, eyes and mouth.

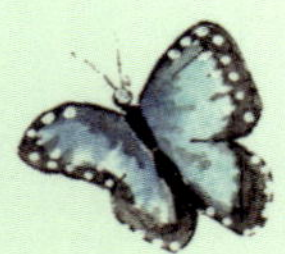

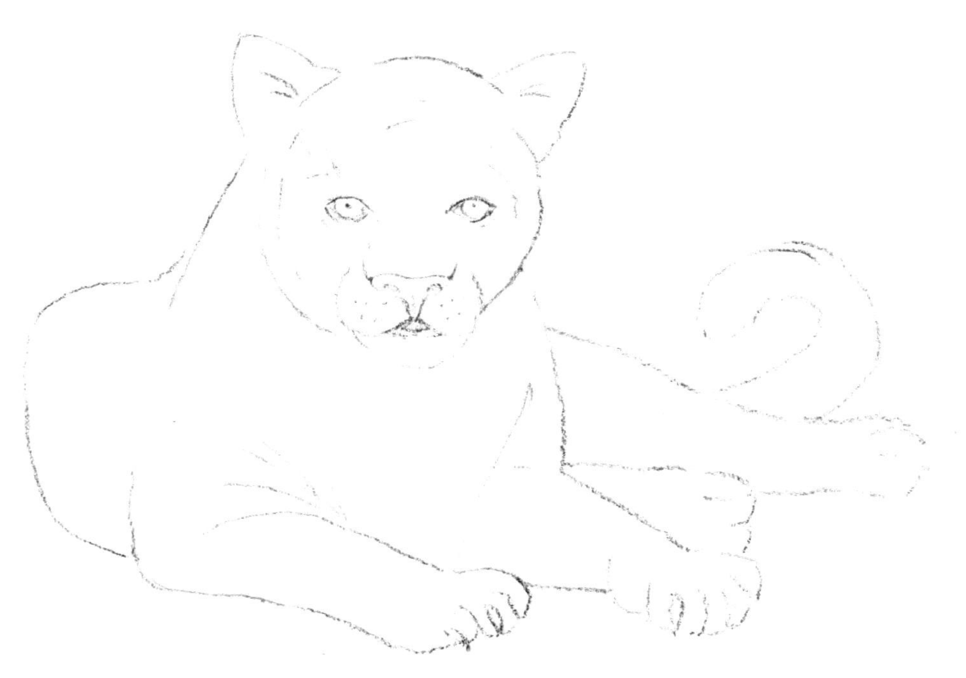

Toucan

That bright orange beak isn't just for show. The massive facial feature also helps to regulate the toucan's temperature. They can adjust the flow of blood to their beaks to warm up, and they even tuck it under their feathers when they sleep to stay cozy!

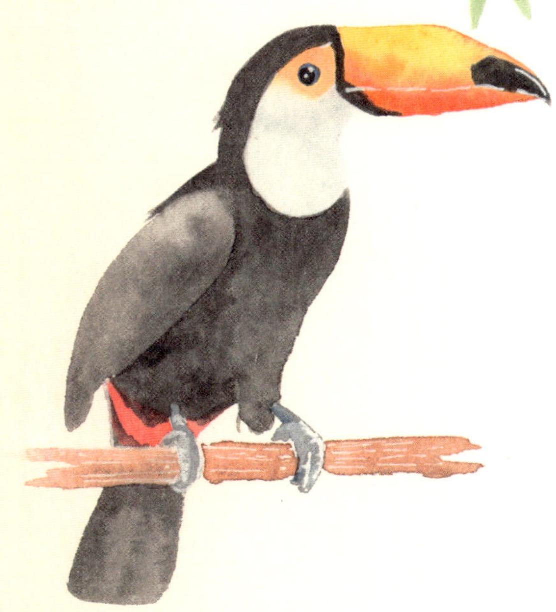

COLOR CHART

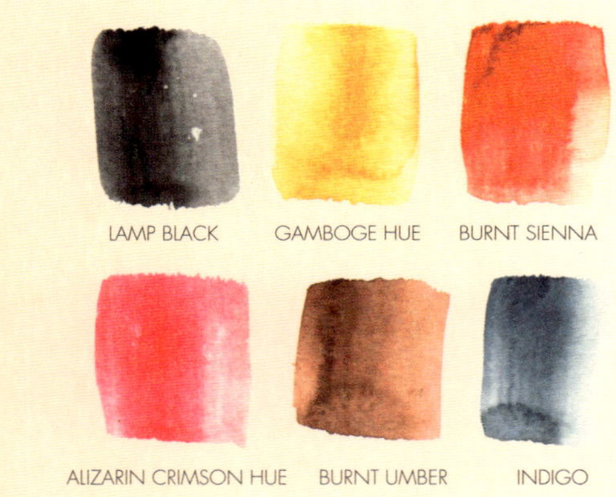

SUPPLIES

- Round brush (size 6 works well)
- Clean water
- 6 colors of paint
- White ink pen

1. Start by dampening the entire black body area (including the tail), leaving the wing free from water. Apply Lamp Black to the whole damp area, allowing the paint to spread out and fill the body.
2. Let that area dry completely. Fill the wing in the same way, using a slightly more watery mix of Lamp Black for a lighter tone.
3. Dampen the beak area with clean water. Apply Gamboge Hue to the entire area, then drop in a little Burnt Sienna to the bottom half, allowing the two colors to blend together. Let dry. Fill in the tip of the beak and eye with Lamp Black.
4. Dampen the area around the eye and neck. Using a tiny amount of Gamboge Hue, add a dab to the top eye area, followed by another light dab of Burnt Sienna.
5. Apply a super diluted mix of Lamp Black to the damp neck area.
6. Fill in the remaining elements as shown in the image with Alizarin Crimson Hue (body stripe), Burnt Umber (tree branch) and Indigo (feet).
7. Use your white ink pen to add highlights to the eyeball, beak and branch, as shown.

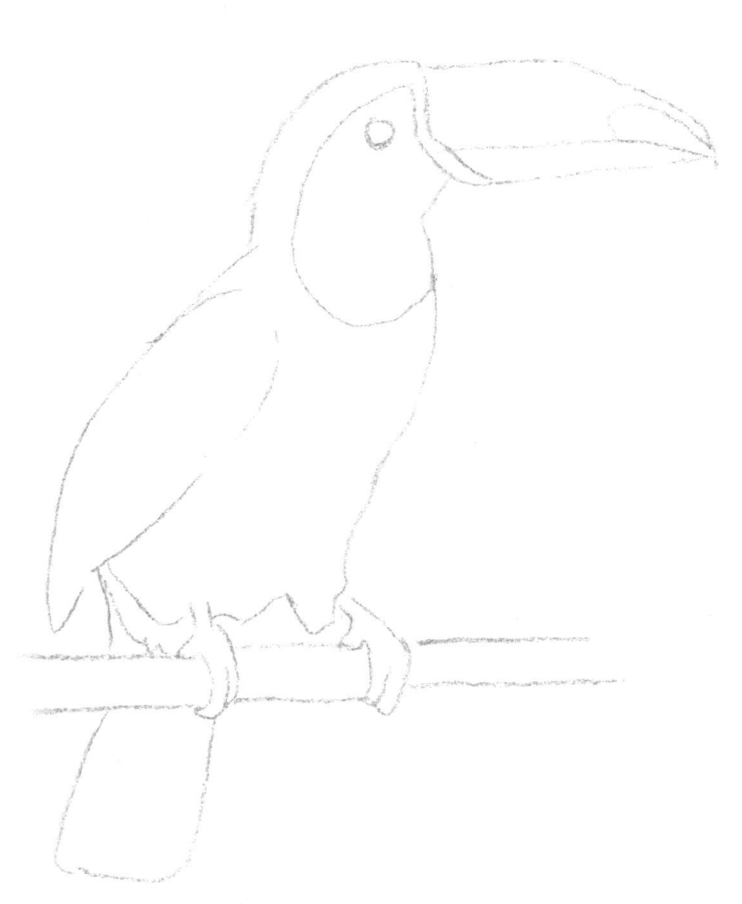

Kinkajou

This cute little guy is also known as the honey bear and lives in the trees of Central and South America.

For this project, you'll start by creating a base layer of wet-on-wet and finish with a fur technique. Be sure to take your time with the fur!

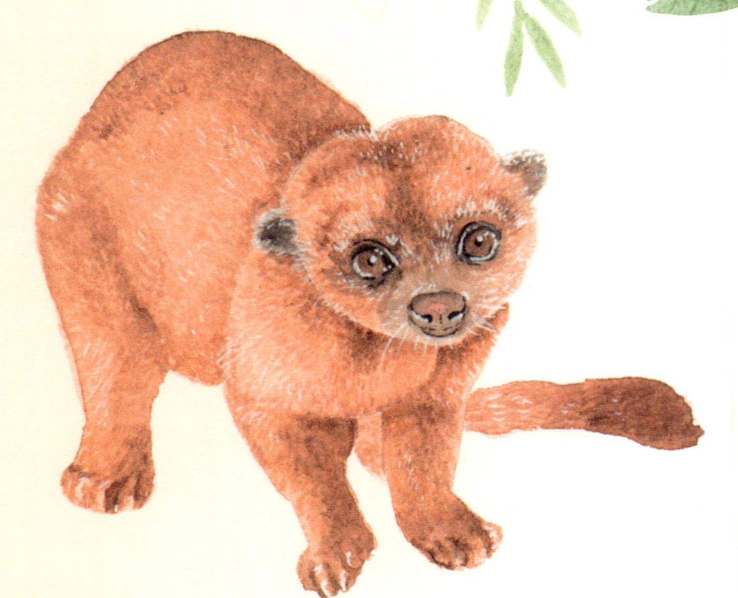

COLOR CHART

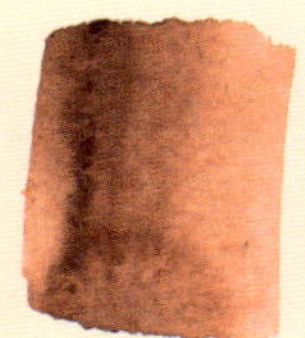

BURNT UMBER

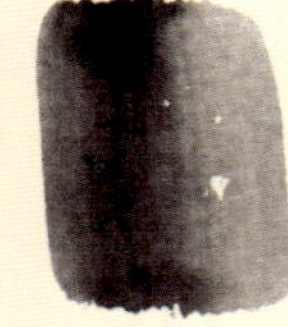

LAMP BLACK

SUPPLIES

- Round brush (size 6 works well)
- Clean water
- 2 colors of paint
- Size 2 or smaller detail brush
- Size 1 black ink pen
- White ink pen

1. Dampen the entire body area of the kinkajou, excluding the head for now. Using a medium tone of Burnt Umber (more water equals a lighter tone!), fill in the entire damp area.
2. While the area is still wet, add a more concentrated (darker) mix of Burnt Umber to some of the shaded areas as shown in the example, such as the feet, end of the tail, top of the back, right side chest and front leg folds. Let dry completely.
3. Use the same technique on the head, darkening the area in between the eyes and on top of the head. Let dry completely.
4. Using the smaller brush, start adding tiny strokes of Burnt Umber all over body. Be sure to keep the direction of fur in mind. Use the sample image for reference. Use lighter mixtures of paint for the lighter areas of fur, and darker ones for the darker areas.
5. Paint the centers of the eyeballs and the nose. Paint the inside of the ears with a light mix of Lamp Black.
6. Once dry, use your black ink pen to draw the lines around the eyes and the nose details. Use the white ink pen to add fur highlights to the body and face. Define the toes with this pen as well.

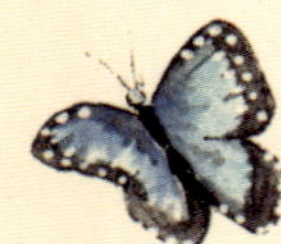

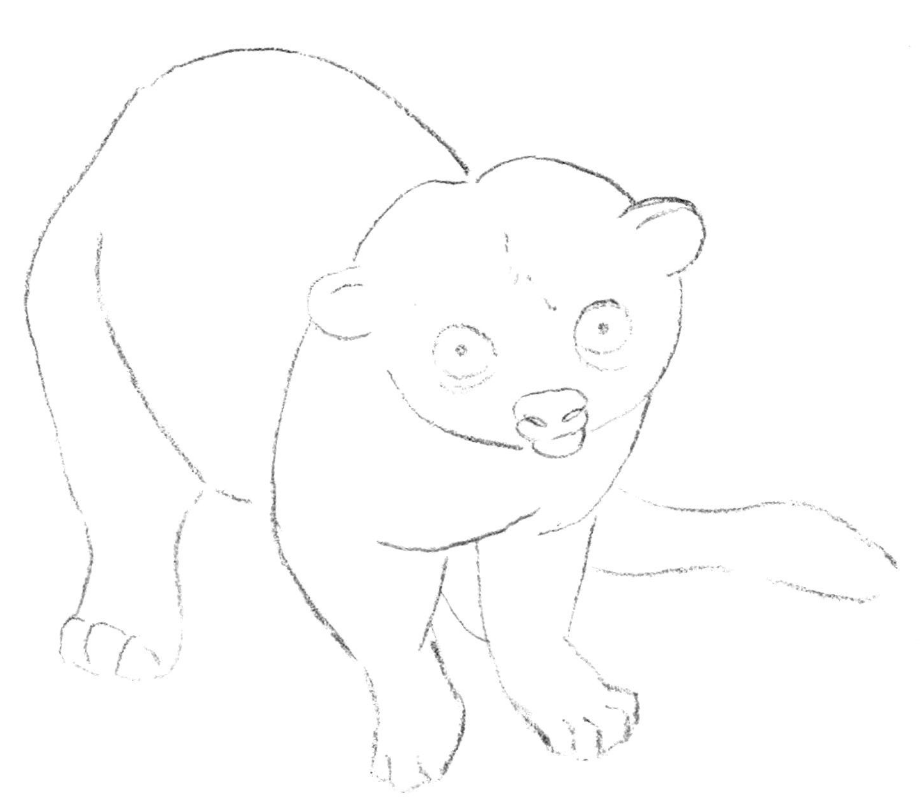

Macaw

These super bright and vibrant birds are large birds of the parrot family. This one in particular is a scarlet macaw and is known to be highly intelligent and quite loud.

The awesome blends on this bird are created by dropping colors into one another.

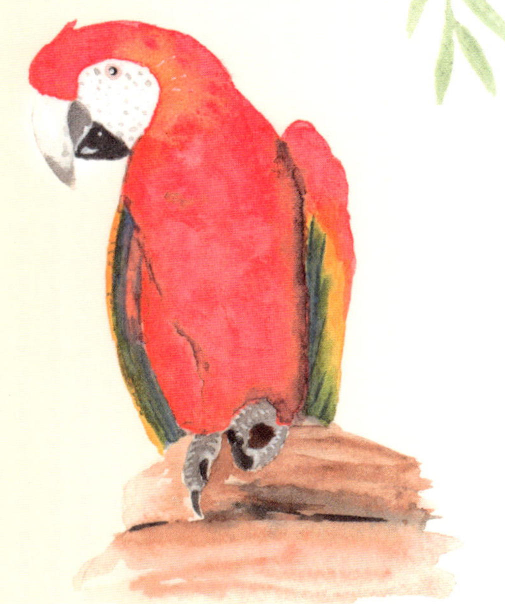

COLOR CHART

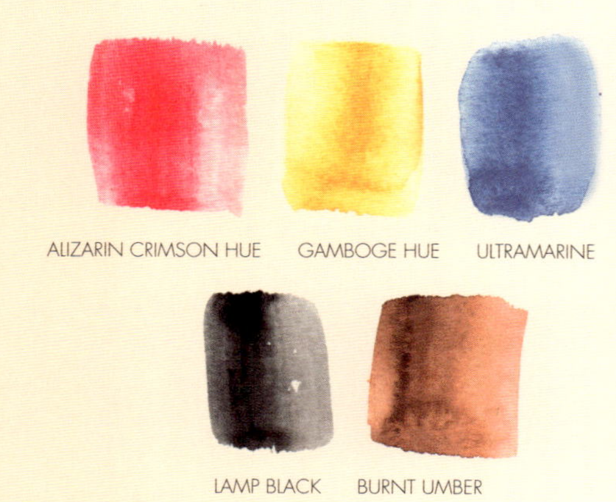

SUPPLIES

- Round brush (size 6 works well)
- Clean water
- 5 colors of paint
- Size 2 or detail brush
- White ink pen

1. Start by using clean water to dampen the red body area of the macaw, avoiding the wings. Apply a concentrated mix of Alizarin Crimson Hue to the entire damp body area.
2. While the area is still wet, add a touch of Gamboge Hue to the side of the head and allow it to blend into the red. Let the body dry, then add Alizarin Crimson Hue to the top of the right wing. Allow to dry.
3. Apply Gamboge Hue to one side of the wing, on both feathers, then add Ultramarine to the other side. Allow them to blend in the center to create a green tone.
4. With a light wash of Lamp Black, fill in the beak, allowing more pigment to collect in the tip. Fill in the mouth area as well, adding more pigment to the bottom section. With your smaller brush, add spots to the face and fill in the eye.
5. Still using Lamp Black, dilute it to a grey shade and paint stripes on the feet. Fill the toenails with a stronger concentration of black.
6. Add Lamp Black along the edge of the body and blend out with a damp brush. Use strokes of Burnt Umber to complete the log.
7. Use the white pen to add highlights to the eyeball, feet and mouth.

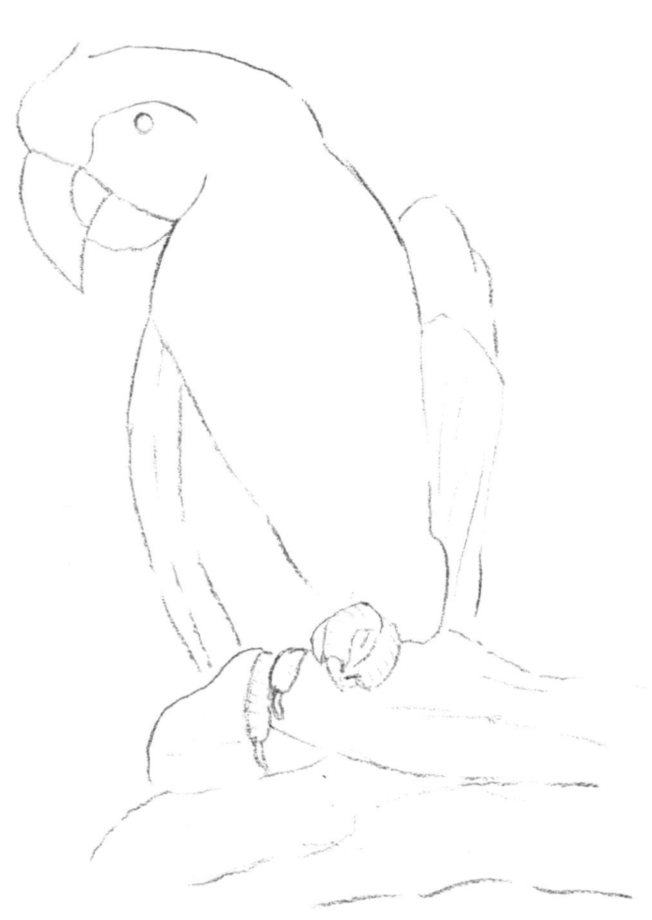

Papaya

This tropical fruit is not only delicious, but the colors are gorgeous, which makes it an ideal subject for a watercolor painting. The colors are created by blending different pigments together on the paper for a loose, implied effect.

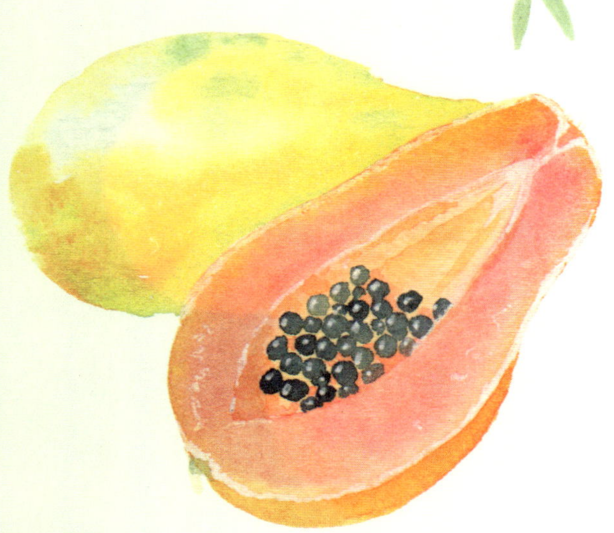

COLOR CHART

ALIZARIN CRIMSON HUE

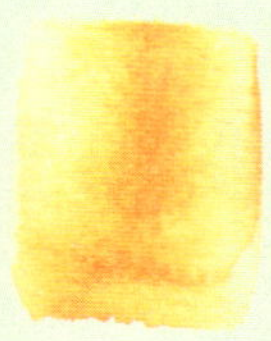
GAMBOGE HUE

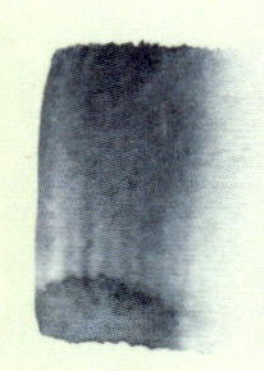
INDIGO

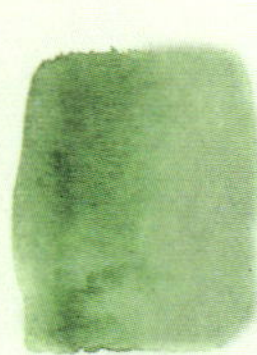
SAP GREEN

SUPPLIES

- Round brush (size 6 works well)
- Clean water
- 4 colors of paint
- White ink pen

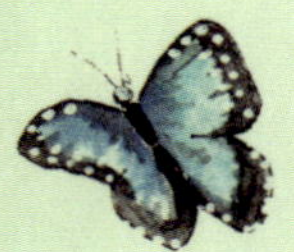

1. Starting with the slice in the front first, wet the edge of the papaya with clean water and drop in a small amount of diluted Alizarin Crimson Hue. Use your brush to coax the paint around the rim.

2. While that part is still wet, apply Gamboge Hue around the outer edges of the slice and let the colors blend together into a nice peachy tone. Let dry.

3. Wet the inside area of the slice, including the seeds. Fill the entire area with Gamboge Hue and then drop in some Alizarin Crimson to darken the bottom interior area below the seeds. Let dry.

4. Use the tip of your brush and Indigo to paint in the seeds.

5. Moving onto the upper slice, fill the entire area with water. Add Gamboge Hue to the whole area, leaving the highlighted area (see sample painting) free from paint.

6. Apply a more concentrated mix of Gamboge Hue to the lower left area to darken it. With a little bit of Sap Green, add a few dots to the wet yellow area.

7. Finally, paint the bottom edge of the first slice with Gamboge Hue and use your white pen to add highlights to the seeds and around the edge of the sliced opening

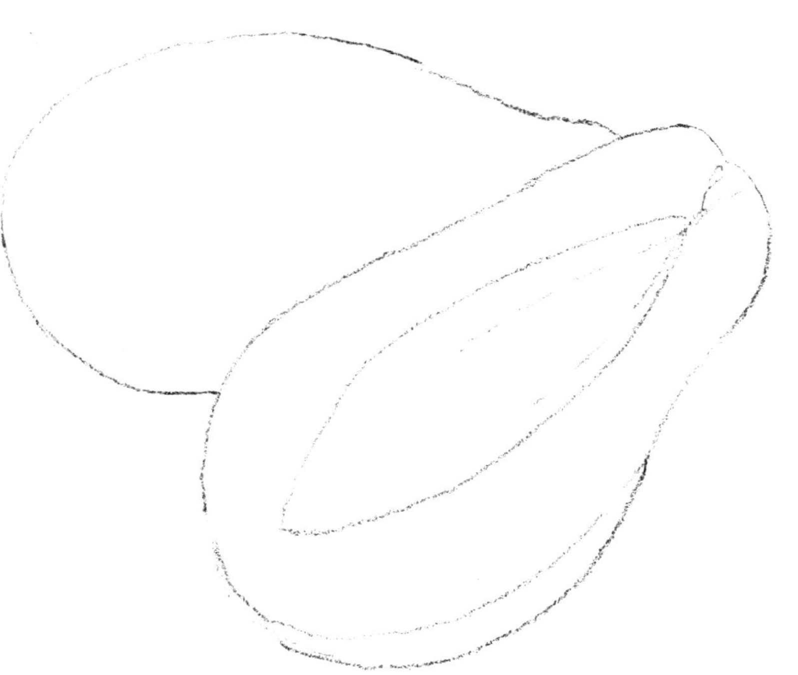

Iguana

These funny creatures can be found lounging in tropical rainforests around the world. They come in many different sizes and colors, but we're going to focus on a bright green version for this project!

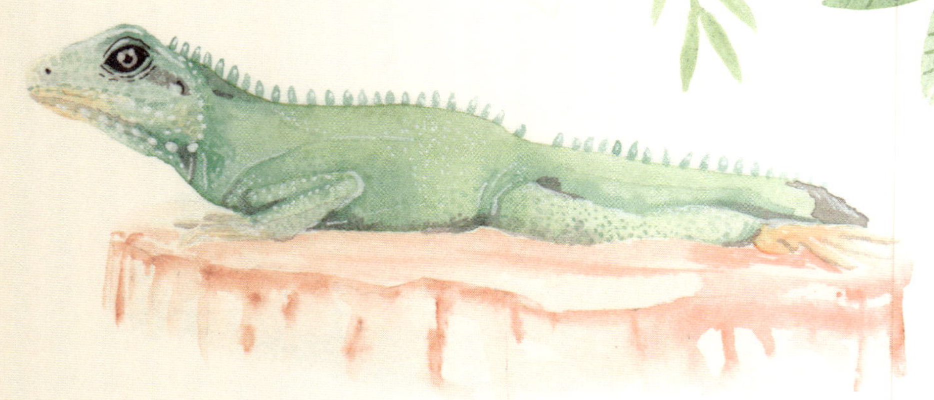

COLOR CHART

SAP GREEN

HOOKER'S DARK GREEN

YELLOW OCHRE

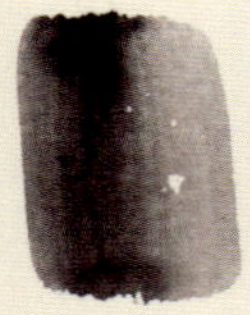

LAMP BLACK

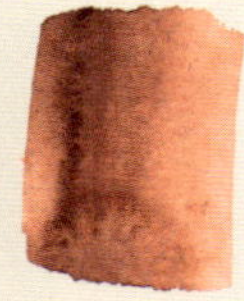

BURNT UMBER

SUPPLIES

- Round brush (size 6 works well)
- Clean water
- 5 colors of paint
- Size 2 or smaller detail brush
- White ink pen
- Size 1 black ink pen

1. Wet the entire body and tail of the iguana, leaving the head and front leg dry for now. Add Sap Green to the damp area and use your brush to coax the paint toward the edges.

2. While the paint is still damp, add Hooker's Dark Green to some of the darker areas for definition, such as around the neck, behind the legs and the belly. Add some Yellow Ochre to the body as well for more interest. Let dry.

3. Fill the head and front leg with water now. Using Sap Green, add a small amount to the face and the leg to fill the area. Using Yellow Ochre, apply just a small amount to the damp area around the front of the face and mouth.

4. Using your smaller brush and Hooker's Dark Green, lightly paint the creases on the body and define the areas around the legs. Use a slightly damp brush to blend any harsh edges.

5. With Lamp Black and your smaller brush, add details to the tip of the tail, the stripe on the face, under the neck, arms and belly. Fill the center of the eye as well.

6. Use the smaller brush with Hooker's Dark Green to paint the spikes along the back and create dots on the face and body for texture.

7. Paint the feet with Yellow Ochre. When dry, add Lamp Black as a shadow below the fingers. Paint the tree stump with quick strokes of Burnt Umber.

8. Finally, use the white ink pen to add dots to the face as shown in the example, as well as highlights on the spikes, dots on the body and highlights in the eye. Use your black ink pen to finish the detail lines around the eye and dot the nostril on.

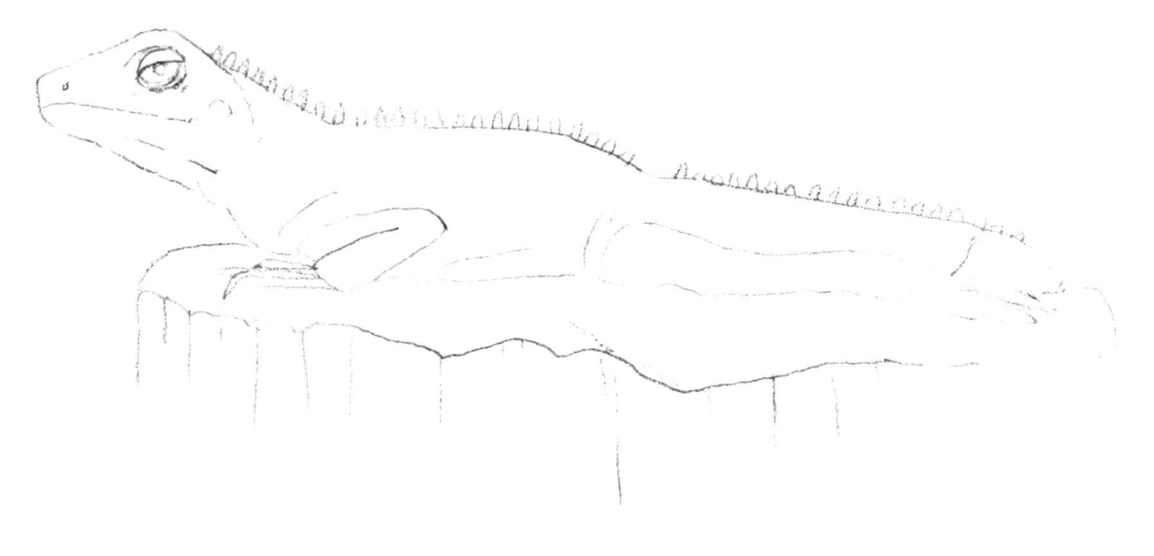

Okapi

This funny looking creature looks like it might stem from a zebra, but it is actually the only living relative of the giraffe. They can be found in rainforests in the Congo. For this project, you'll blend two colors together with water and finish with some sassy stripes!

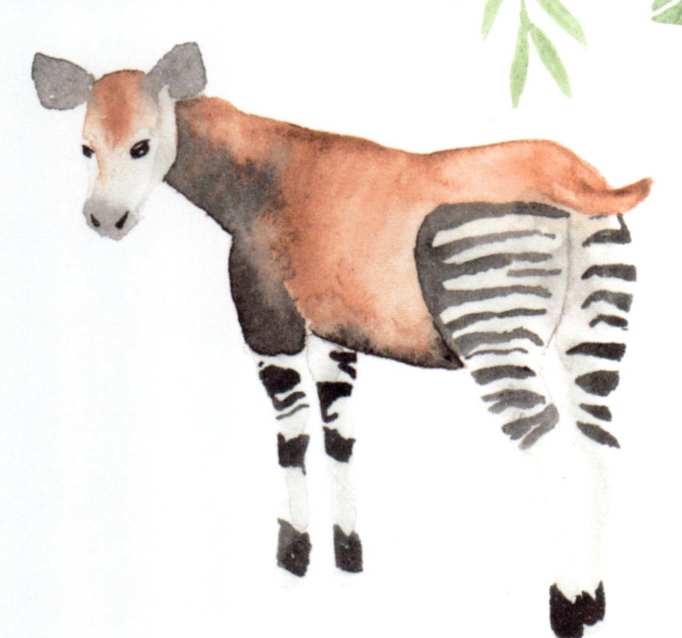

COLOR CHART

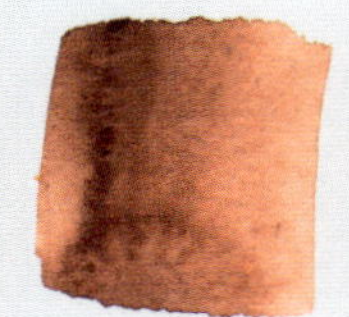

BURNT UMBER

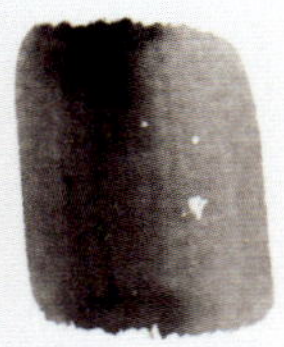

LAMP BLACK

SUPPLIES

- Round brush (size 6 works well)
- Clean water
- 2 colors of paint
- Size 2 or smaller detail brush
- Size 1 black ink pen

1. With clean water only, paint the entire neck and body so the paper is damp.
2. Add dabs of Burnt Umber to the body and move it around to the edges with your brush. Try to avoid the bum area when painting the tail.
3. With the paint still wet, drop in some Lamp Black at the bottom of the neck, front leg and under the belly. Let dry.
4. Wet the legs with clean water and drop in a very diluted shade of Lamp Black. While that dries, wet the head of the okapi and drop in the same diluted grey shade.
5. While the head is still wet, add Burnt Umber to the forehead and allow it to blend downward. Add a more pigmented shade of Lamp Black to the snout and ears and let dry.
6. When the legs are dry, use your smaller brush to paint the stripes and hooves.
7. Use your black ink pen to draw on the eyes and nostrils.

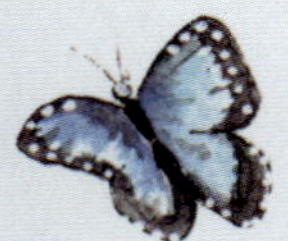

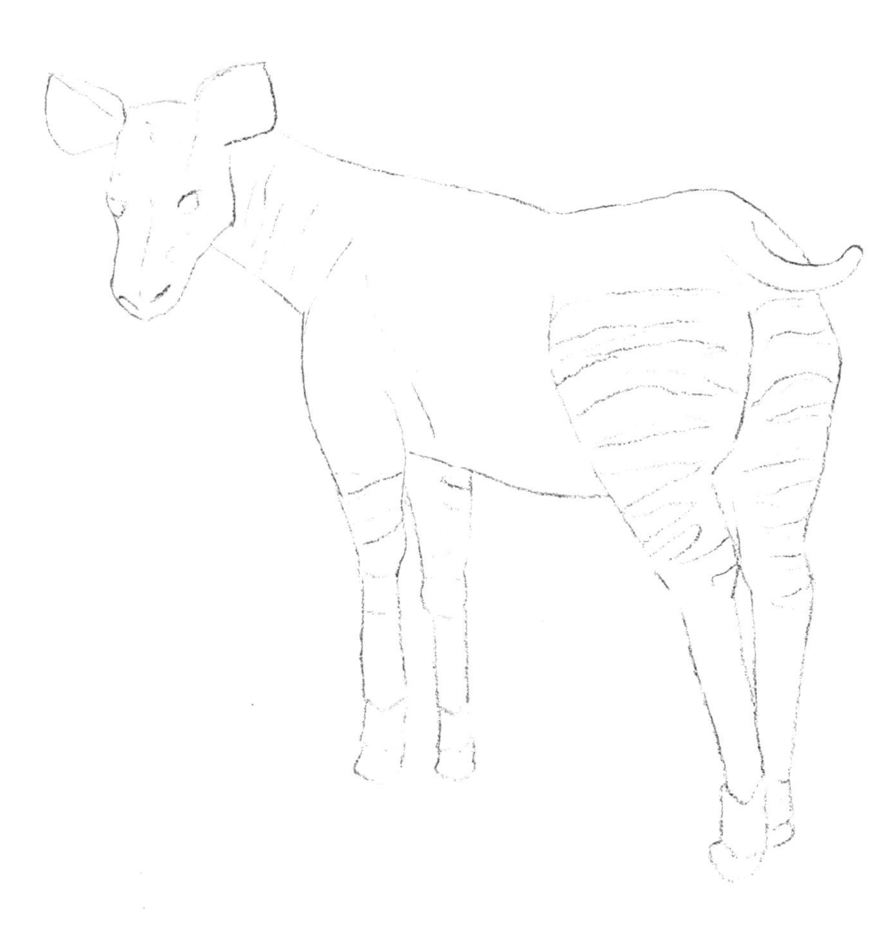

Panda

The only remaining giant pandas in the wild live in a different type of jungle: the bamboo forests of China. While there aren't many left, their population has risen over the past few years, and they are no longer classified as endangered. You just need one color to create this adorable happy guy!

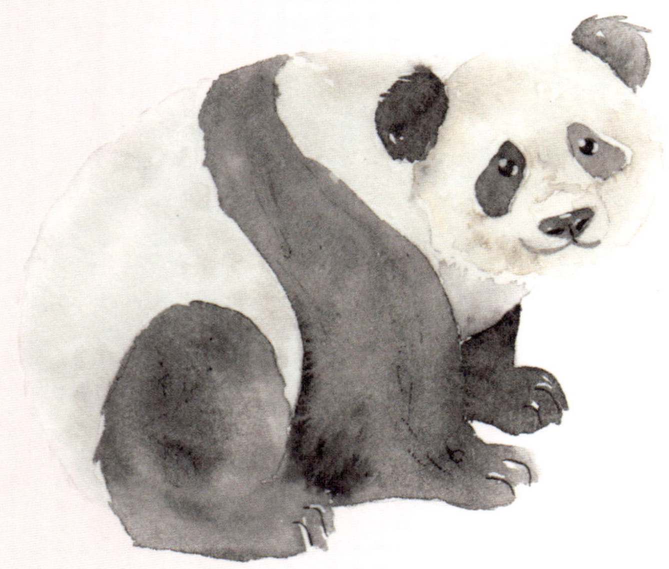

COLOR CHART

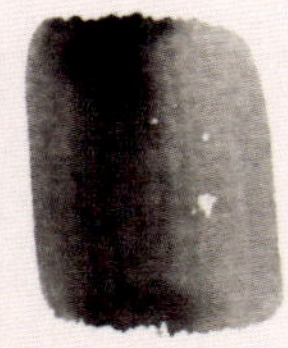

LAMP BLACK

SUPPLIES

- Round brush (size 6 works well)
- Clean water
- 1 color of paint
- Size 1 black ink pen
- White ink pen

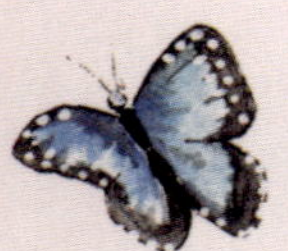

1. You'll paint the black areas first, so start by wetting the legs and black back area with clean water so the paper is damp.
2. Using a pigmented mix of Lamp Black, start dropping the color onto the damp paper. Use the tip of your brush to push the paint to the edges to smooth them out.
3. Wet the ear and eye areas then drop in Lamp Black. Pull out some furry strokes around the ears with the tip of your brush. Paint the nose and mouth onto dry paper.
4. Mix up a very diluted shade of Lamp Black. The color should be a very light grey shade. Apply this color on dry paper to the white areas of the panda.
5. While the white is still damp, add a touch more pigment to the light grey mixture and dab on some darker paint to those areas. Try adding the darker mix to the top of the back, on the face by the ears, in between the eyes, the chest and cheeks. This will just help to add some dimension to the fur.
6. With your black ink pen, draw on the eyes and nostrils. Add lines to the toes to define them.
7. With your white ink pen, add highlights to the eyes, nose and toes.

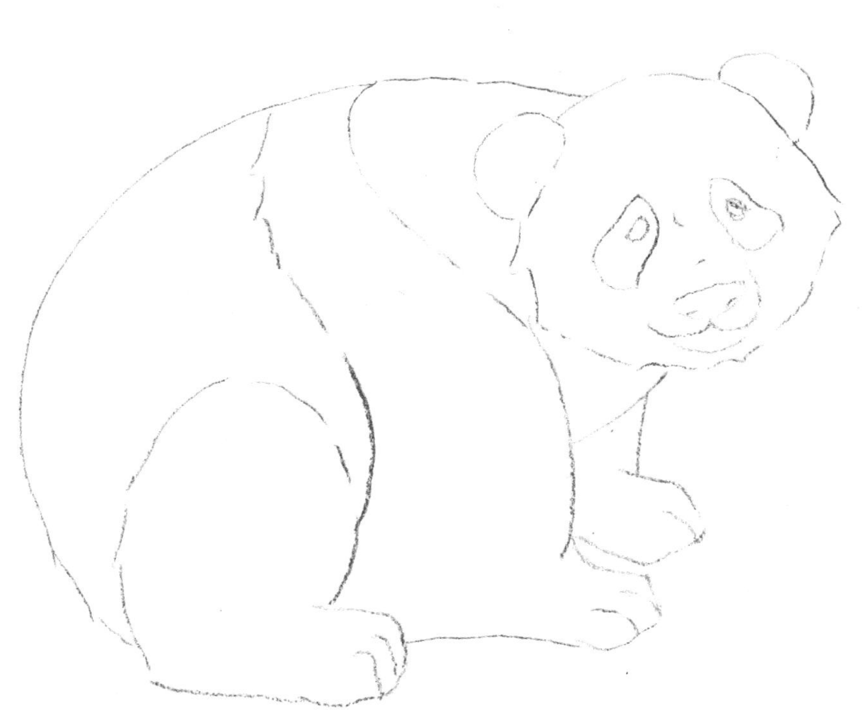

Coconuts

Coconuts are found in tropical areas that get a ton of sunlight and rain. Most coconut palm trees produce about 30 coconuts, which are used for so many different things! These coconuts are created using just two colors and some water!

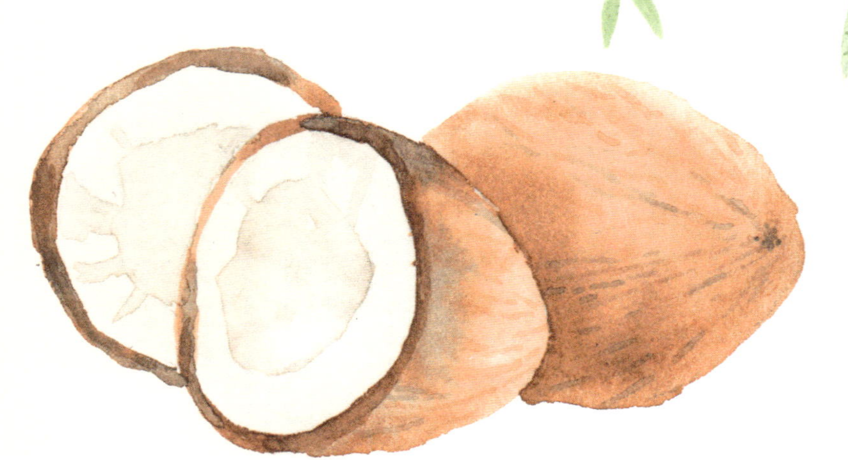

COLOR CHART

RAW UMBER

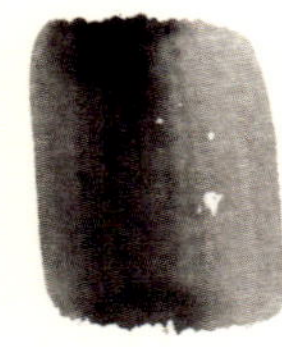

LAMP BLACK

SUPPLIES

- Round brush (size 6 works well)
- Clean water
- 2 colors of paint
- Size 2 or smaller detail brush

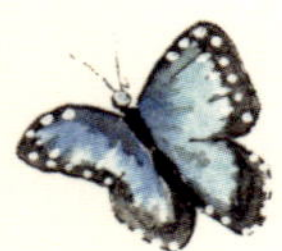

1. Starting with the far-right coconut, wet the entire area with clean water. While the paper is damp, drop in Raw Umber and allow it to fill the space. Use the tip of your brush to push it to the edges if you need to. Add a more pigmented mix of the same color to the edge where the center coconut overlaps. Let dry.

2. Working on the center coconut now, wet the brown skin area with water and drop in Raw Umber. Remember to get the paint around the rim as well! Create darker areas by dropping in Lamp Black. Let dry.

3. Paint the rim of the final coconut with water and then drop in Raw Umber. Add Lamp Black for some darker contrast as well and let dry.

4. Now mix up both Lamp Black with Raw Umber and dilute it with a lot of water to create the shade you see in the center portion of the white areas.

5. Paint the center of the coconuts with this mixture, adding darker dabs around some of the inside edges for contrast. Using your brush, pull some of the color out toward the brown rim.

6. When the piece is dry, use your smaller brush and a medium shade of Raw Umber and Lamp Black to create thin detail lines on the skins of the coconuts.

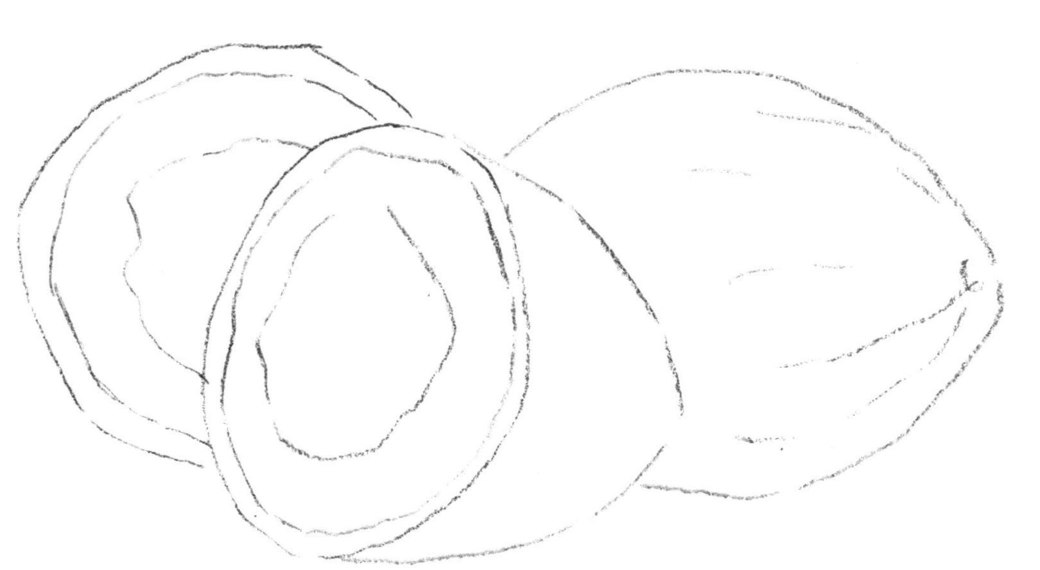

Mandrill

Mandrills—the largest of all monkeys and sometimes called baboons—have super colorful fur with gorgeous blue shades throughout. In this wet-on-wet piece, you'll work in sections and use loose brush strokes to create a sweeping fur effect while blending colors together.

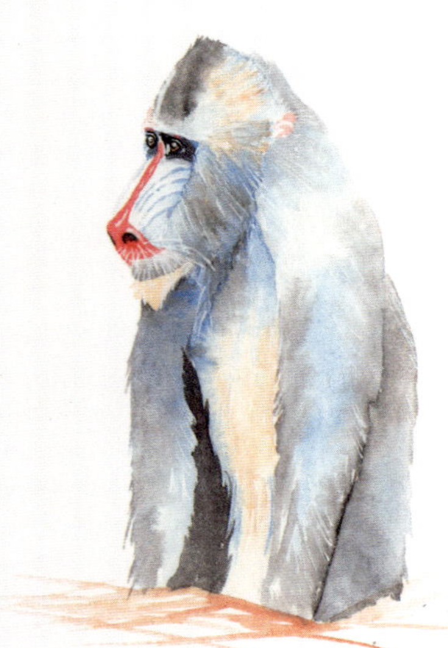

COLOR CHART

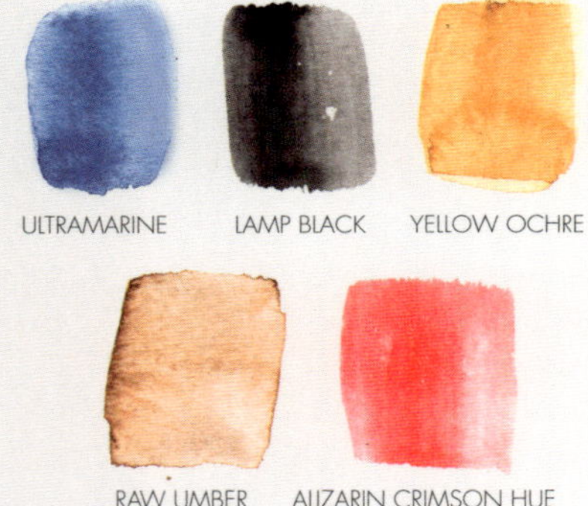

SUPPLIES

- Round brush (size 6 works well)
- Clean water
- Size 2 or smaller detail brush
- 5 colors of paint
- Size 1 black ink pen
- White ink pen

1. Fill the right-hand arm area completely with water. Start dropping in some Ultramarine to the center of the arm and behind the ear. Use the tip of your brush to pull the color down and out toward the edges to create long pieces of fur.

2. Using the same technique, apply Lamp Black to the outside edges of the arm and behind the ear as well. Add a small amount of Yellow Ochre mixed with Raw Umber to the top of the arm where the lightest spot appears on the sample image. Let this area dry completely.

3. Wet the other arm and add Ultramarine to the top area and inner edges. Darken the left-hand side and under the chin with Lamp Black, pulling out long, thin pieces of fur with the tip of your brush as you go. Let dry completely.

4. Wet the chest next and apply Ultramarine to the top and bottom areas, followed by your yellow mix in the center. Always use long strokes for the fur effect! Let dry.

5. Wet the top of the head and side of the face. Referencing the image, add long strokes of Ultramarine, Lamp Black and your yellow mix following the direction of the fur. Add Lamp Black to the top center of the head and let dry completely.

6. With your smaller brush, paint the lines on the face with Ultramarine. Paint the nose and ear with Alizarin Crimson Hue. Paint the chin hair with the yellow mix, and fill the surrounding eye area with a dark mix of Ultramarine. Fill the space beside the arm with Lamp Black and use Raw Umber to sweep on some branches below the mandrill.

7. Use your black ink pen to fill in the eyeballs and nostril, then use the white pen to add highlights to the nose, eyes and moustache, and add additional strokes throughout the fur.

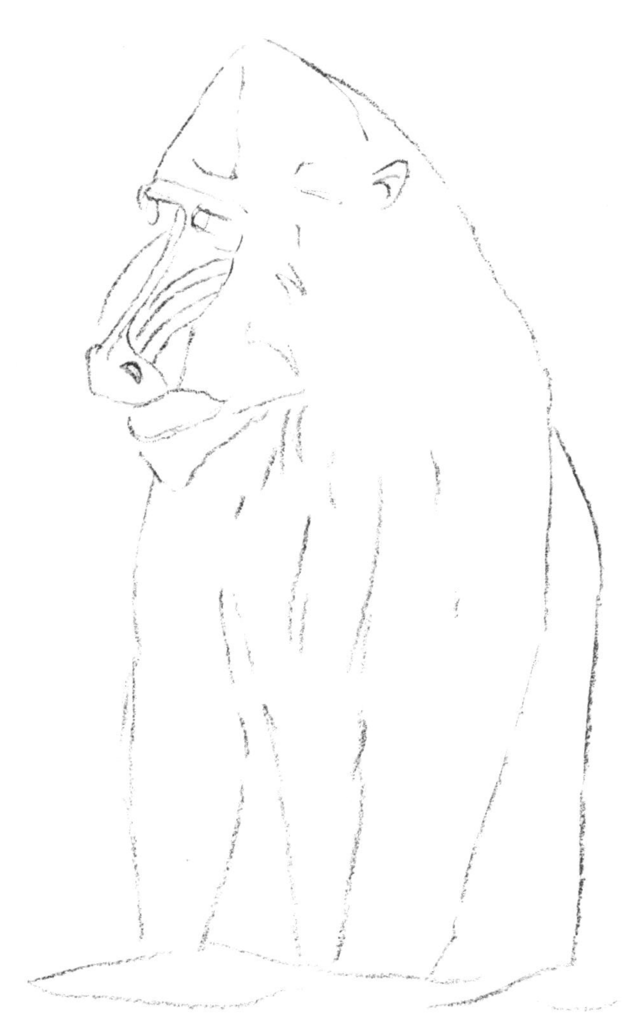

Figs

These colorful fruits are an important part of the ecosystem in tropical forests, as they feed many critters and wildlife.

The loose look of this piece will give you some classic watercolor charm!

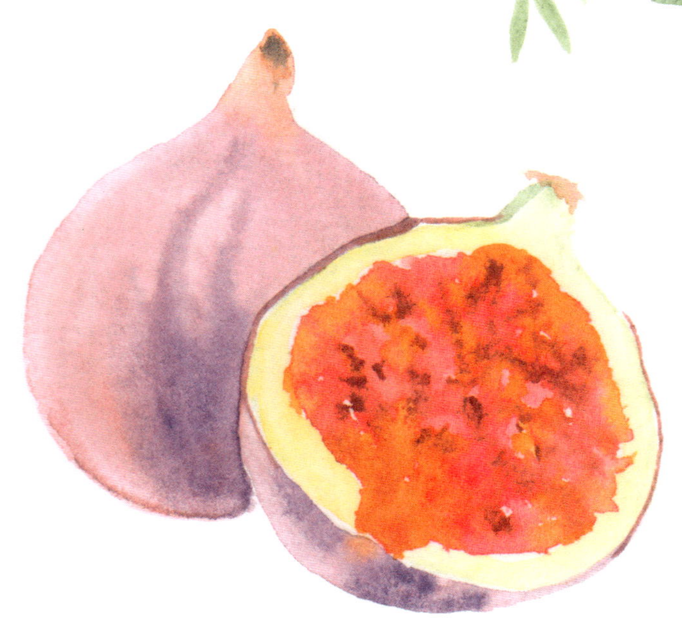

COLOR CHART

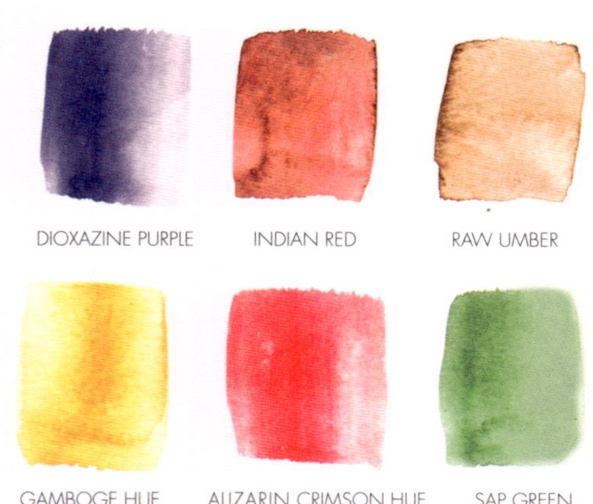

SUPPLIES

- Round brush (size 6 works well)
- Clean water
- 6 colors of paint

1. Starting with the fig in the back, fill the entire shape with water. Mix a little Dioxazine Purple and Indian Red to create a plum shade. Apply this color to the wet paper. Use your brush tip to smooth out the edges.
2. While still wet, swipe on Dioxazine Purple in a streaky motion to create some darker lines on the fig.
3. Apply a bit of Raw Umber to the top stem of the fig and let it dry.
4. Fill the interior rim of the sliced fig with water and add Gamboge Hue with your brush. Let dry.
5. Wet the bottom of the sliced fig and drop in your plum mixture and some Dioxazine Purple and let dry.
6. Fill the entire center of the open fig with water and start dotting in spots of Alizarin Crimson Hue. Then dot in Indian Red while it's still wet, followed by Gamboge Hue. Allow the colors to blend.
7. Finish by outlining the skin of the open fig with your plum mix, followed by a little Sap Green at the top stem area. Add Raw Umber to the top of the stem, and darken the other stem with the same color.

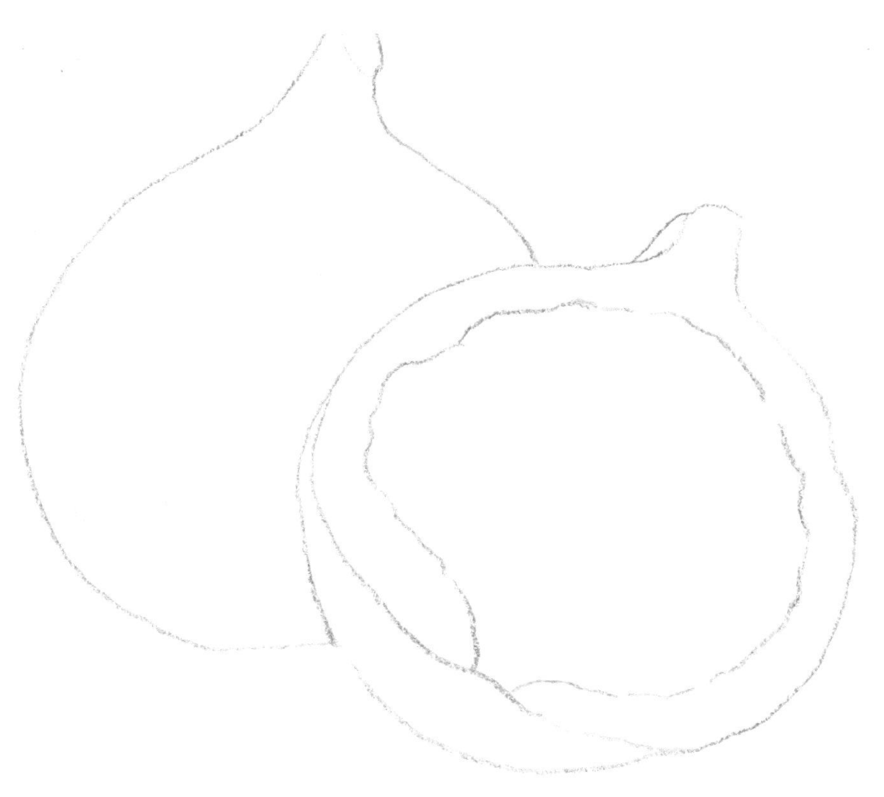

Jewel Beetle

The iridescence of this bug is simply stunning, and you'll get a chance to recreate it with some gorgeous blends of blues and greens. Highlighting becomes an important step in giving this beetle texture and shine. You'll use a stippling technique to finish this piece.

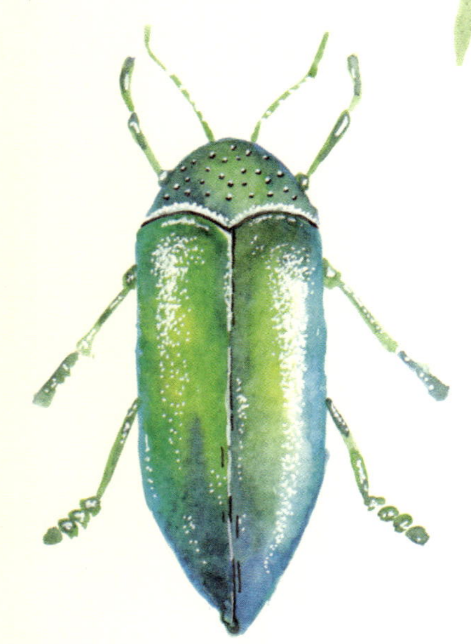

COLOR CHART

CERULEAN BLUE HUE

GAMBOGE HUE

SAP GREEN

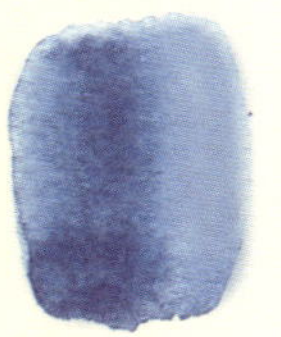

ULTRAMARINE

SUPPLIES

- Round brush (size 6 works well)
- Clean water
- 4 colors of paint
- White ink pen
- Size 1 black ink pen

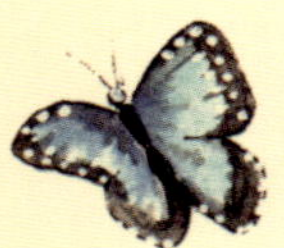

1. Wet only one side of the back of the beetle to begin. On the damp paper, add Cerulean Blue Hue to the outside edges and allow it to move toward the center.

2. While that color is still wet, add a little Gamboge Hue to the center and allow it to mix with the blue shade to create a green. Add a little extra green to the yellow areas using Sap Green. Finally, use Ultramarine around the outside edges to darken the blue. Use your brush to help mix the colors on the paper. Let dry.

3. Repeat the same steps on the opposite side.

4. Fill the head area with water and drop in Cerulean Blue Hue around the edges once again, followed by Gamboge Hue in the center and Sap Green on top of that. Let blend and allow to dry.

5. Paint the antennae, arms and legs with Sap Green. Dot on some Ultramarine to the wider parts. Let dry.

6. Using your white ink pen, start stippling on some highlights to the back of the beetle. The whitest parts should contain more dense dots, allowing them to trail off and separate more as the highlight becomes less intense.

7. Highlight the lines on the body, arms and head and add dots to the face with the white ink pen. With your black ink pen, add shadow detail below the white lines and the dots on the head.

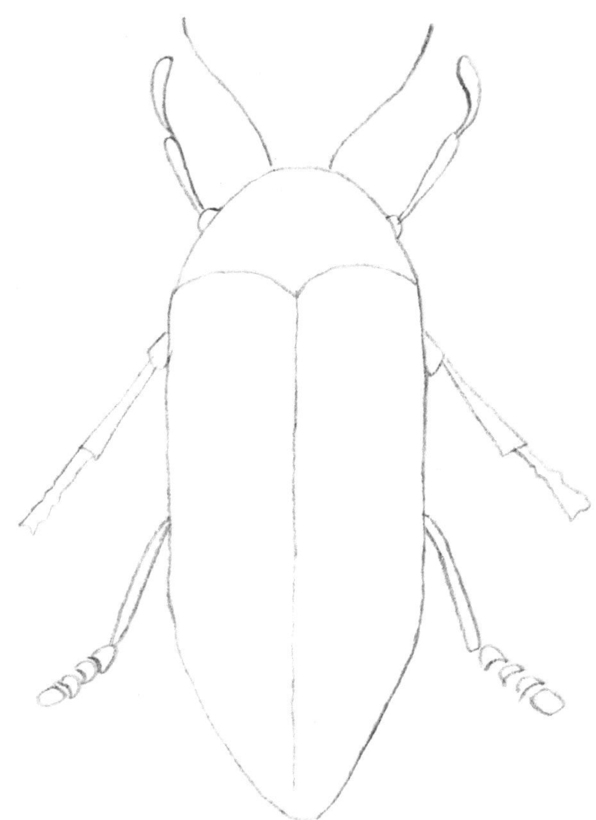

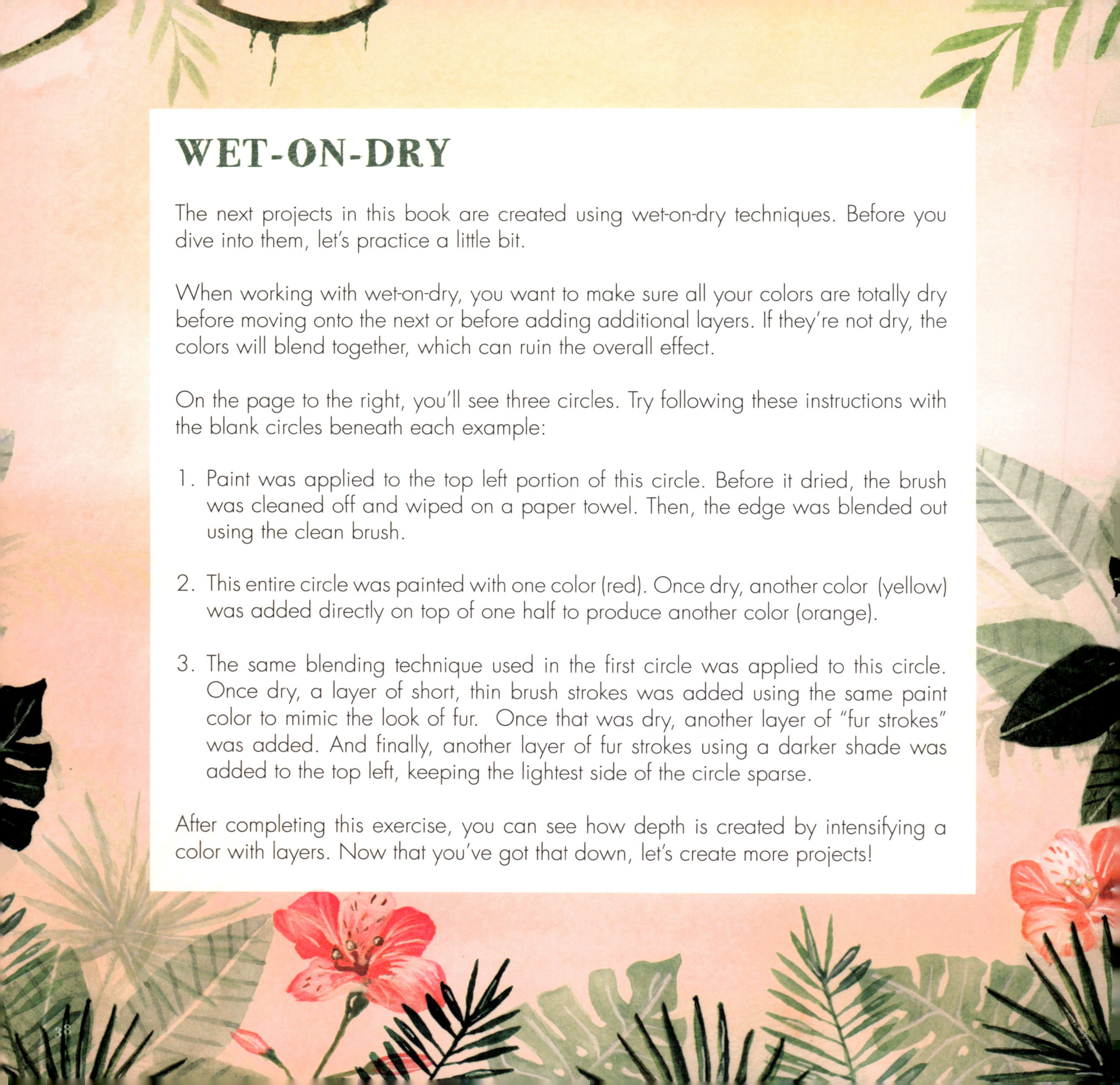

WET-ON-DRY

The next projects in this book are created using wet-on-dry techniques. Before you dive into them, let's practice a little bit.

When working with wet-on-dry, you want to make sure all your colors are totally dry before moving onto the next or before adding additional layers. If they're not dry, the colors will blend together, which can ruin the overall effect.

On the page to the right, you'll see three circles. Try following these instructions with the blank circles beneath each example:

1. Paint was applied to the top left portion of this circle. Before it dried, the brush was cleaned off and wiped on a paper towel. Then, the edge was blended out using the clean brush.

2. This entire circle was painted with one color (red). Once dry, another color (yellow) was added directly on top of one half to produce another color (orange).

3. The same blending technique used in the first circle was applied to this circle. Once dry, a layer of short, thin brush strokes was added using the same paint color to mimic the look of fur. Once that was dry, another layer of "fur strokes" was added. And finally, another layer of fur strokes using a darker shade was added to the top left, keeping the lightest side of the circle sparse.

After completing this exercise, you can see how depth is created by intensifying a color with layers. Now that you've got that down, let's create more projects!

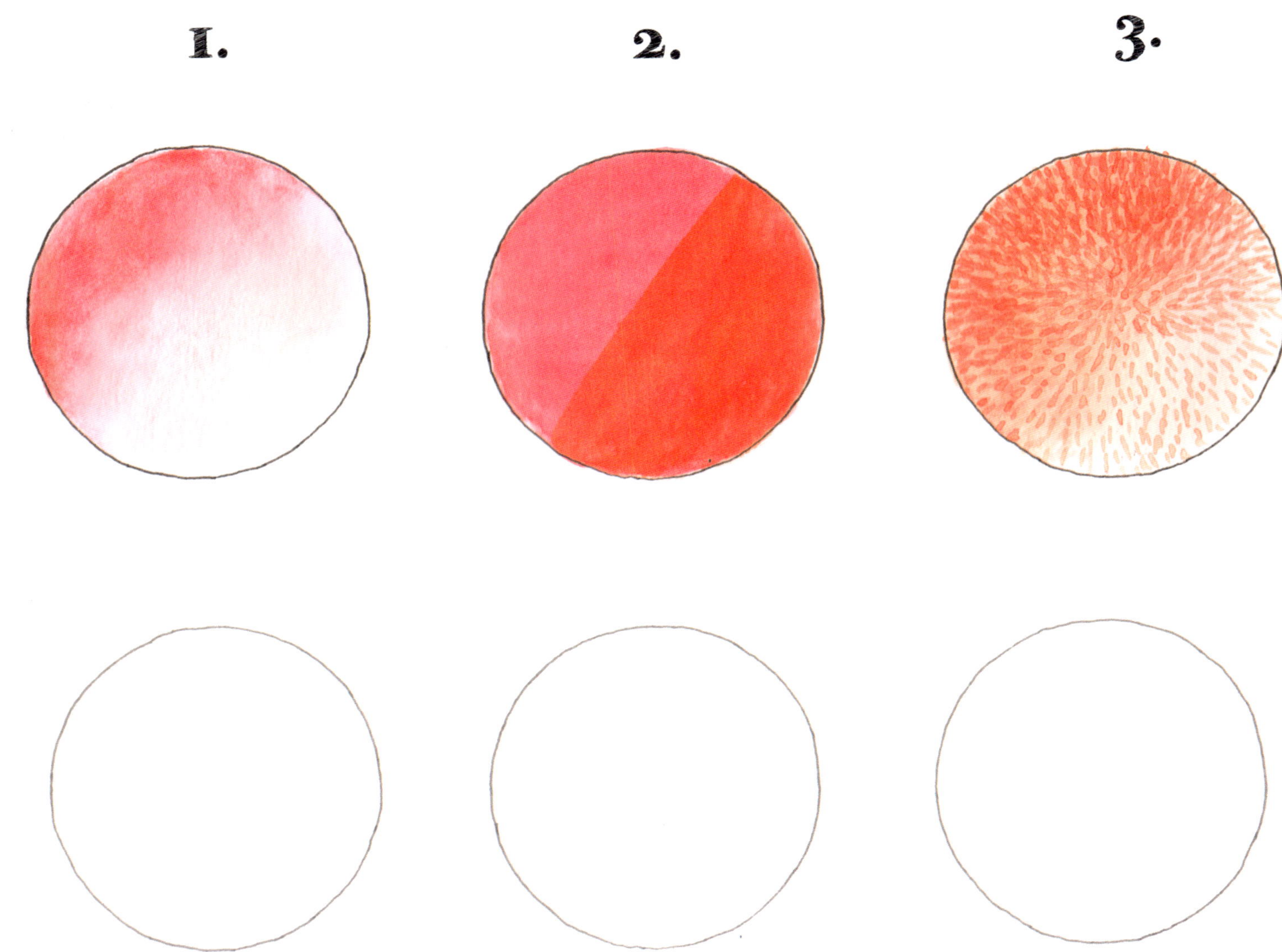
1.
2.
3.

Sloth

This slow-moving sloth is the laziest mammal in the jungle, and he likes to spend his time hanging upside down from the trees. Let's capture his personality and that long, algae-covered fur coat. The white ink pen will complete this piece, so be sure to have one handy!

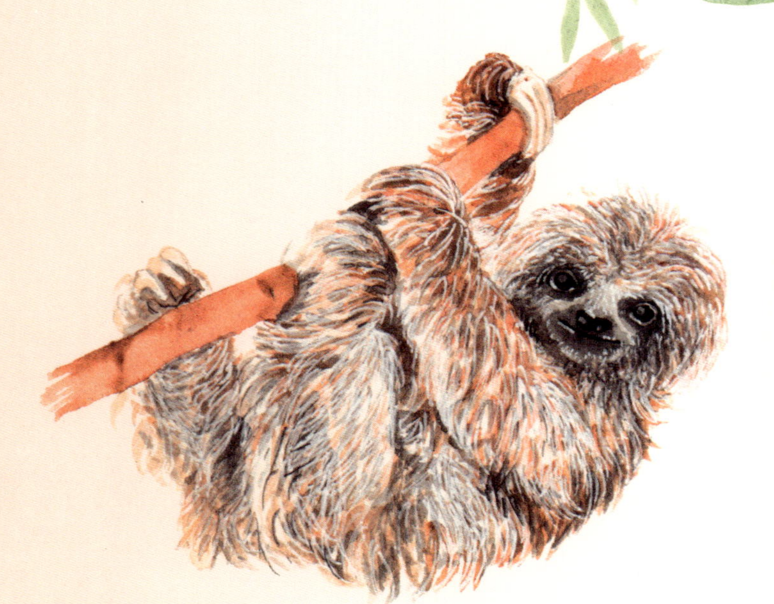

COLOR CHART

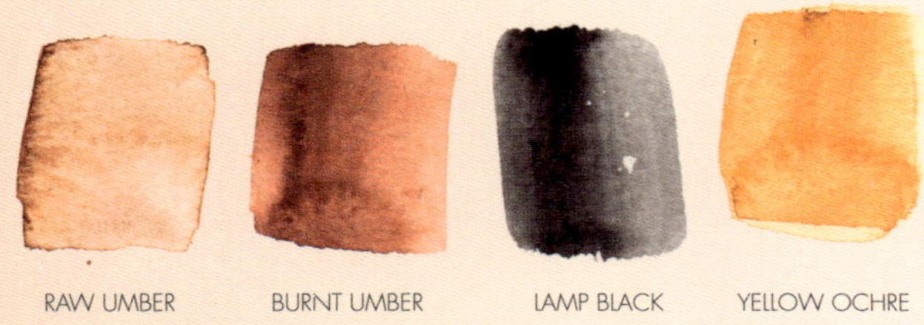

SUPPLIES

- Round brush (size 2 works well)
- 4 colors of paint
- Clean water
- Size 1 black ink pen
- White ink pen

1. Instead of painting a solid base, we're going to paint this entire sloth with single strokes of the brush to mimic fur. Starting with a light shade of Raw Umber, paint the fur on the top arm, stroke by stroke. Remember to follow the direction of the arm and curves.

2. Continue painting the rest of the body using these single strokes and following the direction of the fur, as shown in the sample image. We'll do the head last.

3. When that layer is dry, continue adding fur with Burnt Umber, followed by Lamp Black in the darkest areas and Yellow Ochre in the lightest areas for a sunlit glow.

4. Paint the face with a very light wash of Lamp Black and let it dry. Then paint around the eyes, nose and mouth with a darker mixture of Lamp Black Follow the curves of the head and paint shorter strokes in layers of color as you did on the body.

5. Paint the fingernails with a light wash of Raw Umber and Yellow Ochre. Paint the tree branch with Burnt Umber.

6. Fill in the eyes and nose with your black ink pen, and draw on the mouth. Using your white ink pen, start adding even more long strokes of fur on top of the painted fur for highlights. Add more to the lighter areas and be sure to do the same around the face.

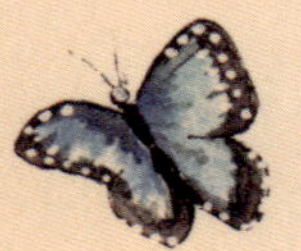

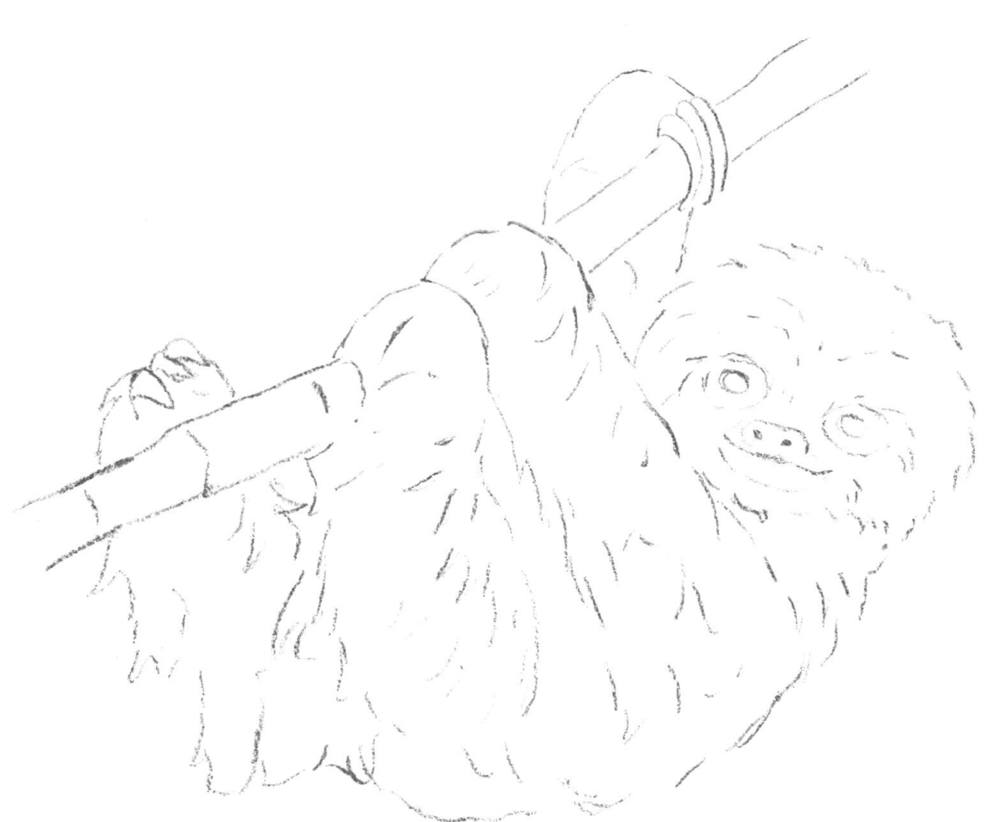

Forest Elephant

This sweet guy is native to humid African rainforests and helps to germinate many trees. The majority of this project is created using just one paint color with varying levels of water.

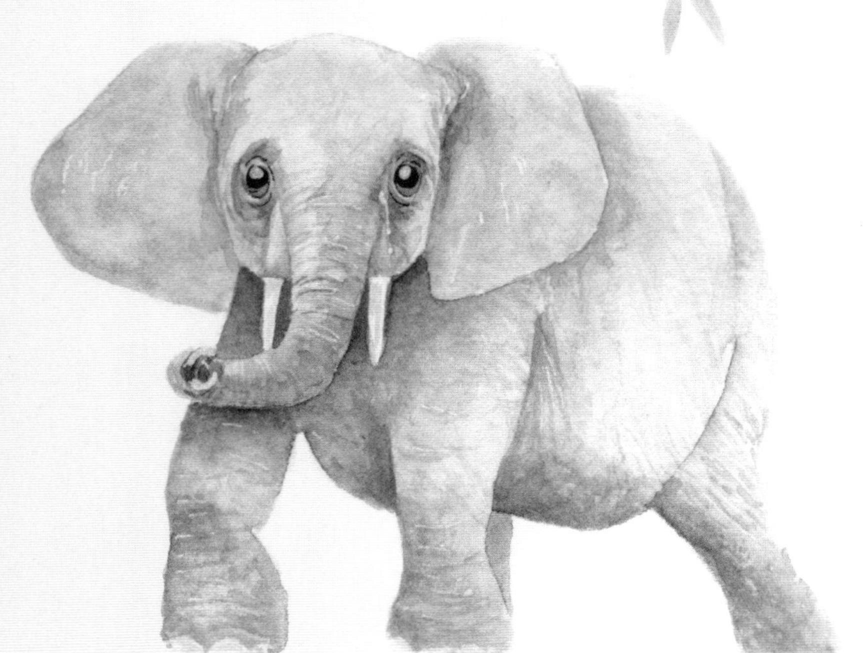

COLOR CHART

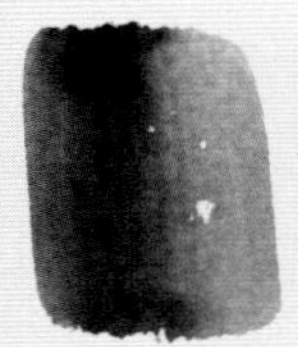

LAMP BLACK

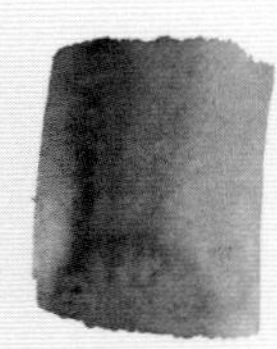

BURNT UMBER

SUPPLIES

- Round brush (size 6 works well)
- 2 colors of paint
- Clean water
- Size 2 or smaller detail brush
- Size 1 black ink pen
- White ink pen

1. Start with the right hand side of the body, behind the front leg, including the back leg. Mix Lamp Black with about 50 percent water to create light grey. Paint the entire area with this shade and let dry.

2. Move on to the chest area and front legs, filling the whole area with the same shade of grey. Finally, complete the entire head in the same way. This is your base layer. Let dry.

3. With a slightly more pigmented shade of grey, start adding in the darker shaded areas as shown on the sample—under the belly, the back foot, the chest, behind the ear, on the face and around the neck. Use a slightly damp brush to blend out any harsh edges.

4. Darken the areas around the eyes and tusks, using your smaller brush to create any wrinkles and outlines on the face. Use this same brush to create wrinkles on the trunk, legs and throughout the body as shown.

5. Use a little bit of Burnt Umber to fill in the eyes and trunk hole. Dilute it to a light wash and fill in the tusks.

6. Finally, use your black ink pen to finish the details on the eyeballs. Use the white ink pen to add highlights to the eyes and some of the wrinkles throughout the body.

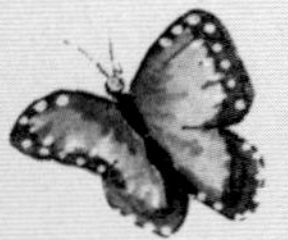

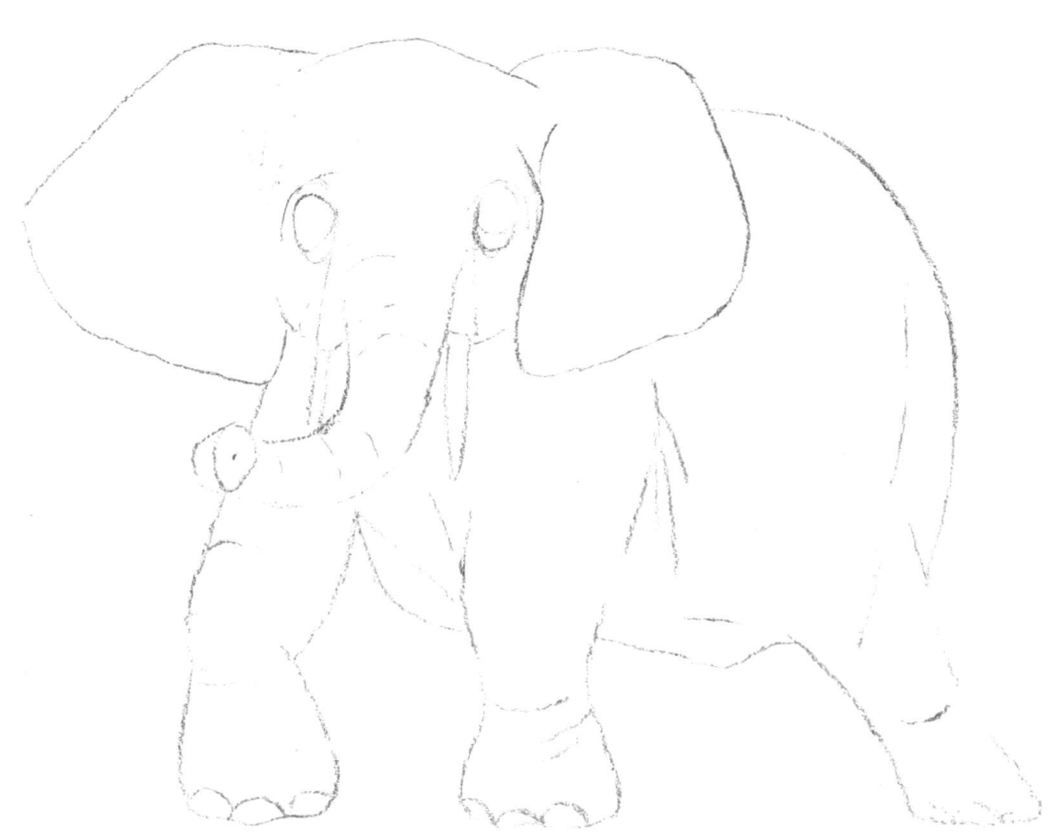

Golden Lion Tamarin

This endangered species is known for its thick mane and resides in the Atlantic Forest. In this project, you'll recreate its long, lush fur by spending time working with thin brushstrokes.

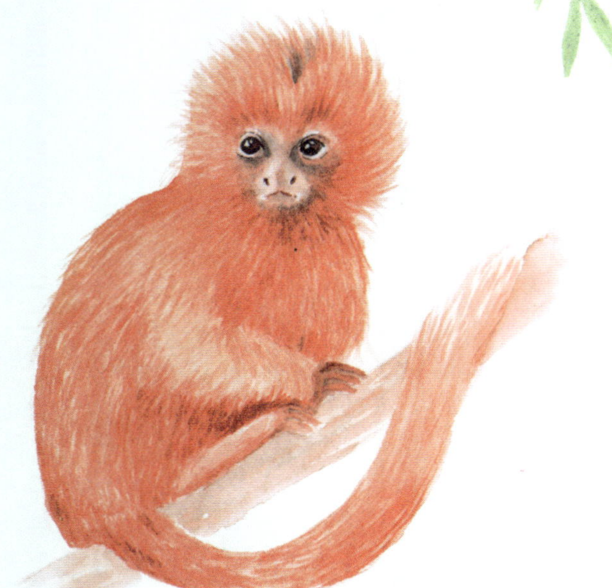

COLOR CHART

BURNT SIENNA

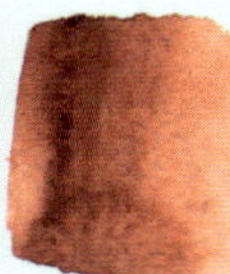
BURNT UMBER

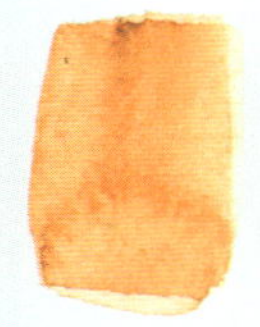
YELLOW OCHRE

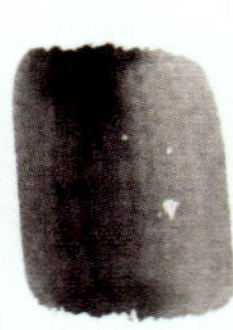
LAMP BLACK

SUPPLIES

- Round brush (size 6 works well)
- 4 colors of paint
- Clean water
- Size 2 or smaller detail brush
- Size 1 black ink pen
- White ink pen

1. Start by filling in the entire body with a 50/50 mixture of Burnt Sienna and Burnt Umber mixed with water, being sure not to paint the hairless face.
2. Once that layer is dry, use your smaller brush to fill in the body with long, swift brush strokes. To begin, start with a more diluted mixture of Burnt Sienna and Burnt Umber and create brush strokes all over the body, being sure to keep the direction of your strokes in line with the curves of the body.
3. Once that has dried, add another layer of fur strokes, concentrating on some of the midtone and darker areas of the animal. The more you layer, the darker those areas will appear.
4. For your final layer of fur, concentrate on darkening the shaded areas with more Burnt Umber. Apply a light layer of Yellow Ochre strokes over the whole body for a sunlit effect.
5. Moving onto the head, apply the same layering technique and mimic the direction of fur as in the sample image. Add a little bit of Lamp Black to the top center of the head.
6. For the face, mix up a very diluted shade of Burnt Umber and paint the whole area. Let dry and darken the area under the eyes using a darker mix of Burnt Umber, allowing the nose to stand out. Use the same mixture to paint the tree branch and a darker mixture to paint the hand.
7. With your black ink pen, carefully fill in the eyes and detail lines around the eyes. Add the nostrils and mouth. Use the white pen to add highlights to the eyes and facial features.

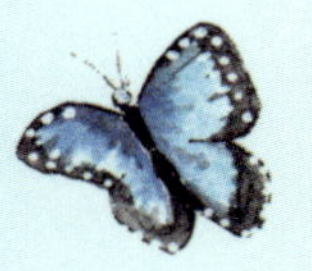

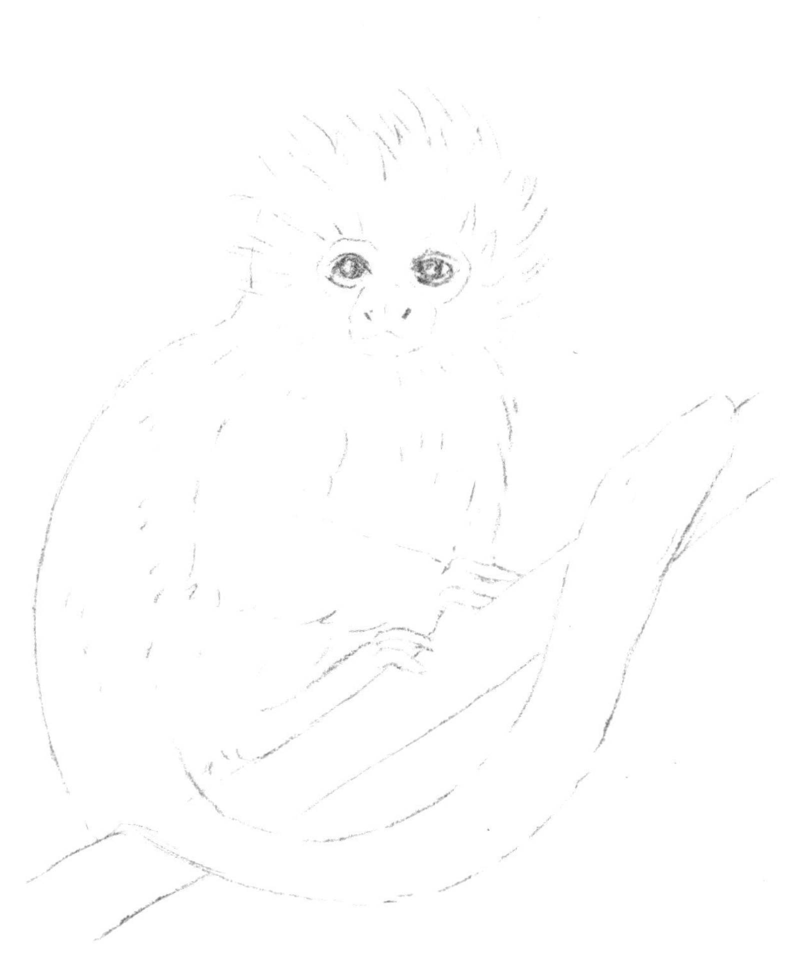

Harpy Eagle

As the most powerful of birds, this eagle flies below the forest canopy and can crush its prey with 100 pounds of force in its talons. Let's paint one using quick brush strokes and a muted color palette.

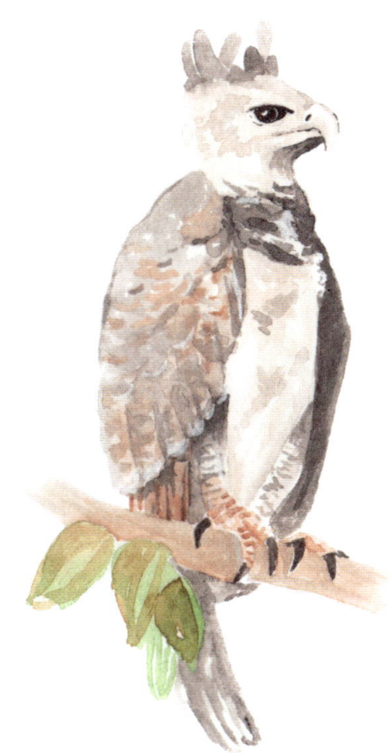

COLOR CHART

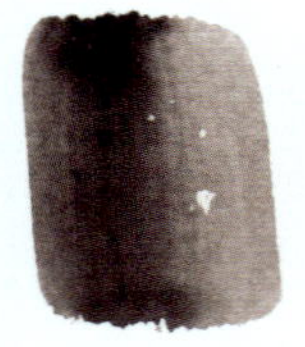

LAMP BLACK

BURNT UMBER

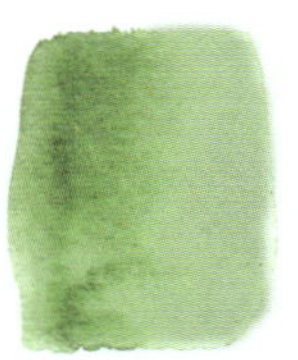

SAP GREEN

SUPPLIES

- Round brush (size 6 works well)
- 3 colors of paint
- Clean water
- Size 1 black ink pen

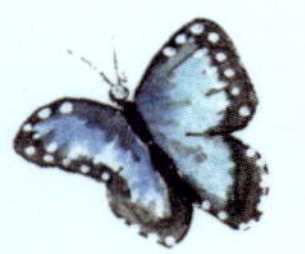

1. Start by mixing up a diluted shade of Lamp Black to create a light grey. Apply this color to the head of the eagle using short, swift strokes, allowing some of the paper to show through. Do the same on the white chest area and the beak of the bird.

2. With a more pigmented shade of the grey you mixed up, apply more swift strokes to the neck area, leaving some of the white poking through. Paint the right-hand wing, toenails, tail, under-the-mouth shadow and head feathers as well.

3. For the left-hand wing, use a medium tone Lamp Black mixture and fill the area with short strokes again. Add in some Burnt Umber as well. To define the feathers, use a darker mix of Lamp Black and apply it under some of the outlines on the wing.

4. Paint the feet with a light wash of Burnt Umber. Once dry, add stripes to the feet with the same color. Paint the tree branch too.

5. With Sap Green, paint the leaves then add Burnt Umber on top.

6. Using your black ink pen, fill in and outline the eyeball, mouth and ncstril.

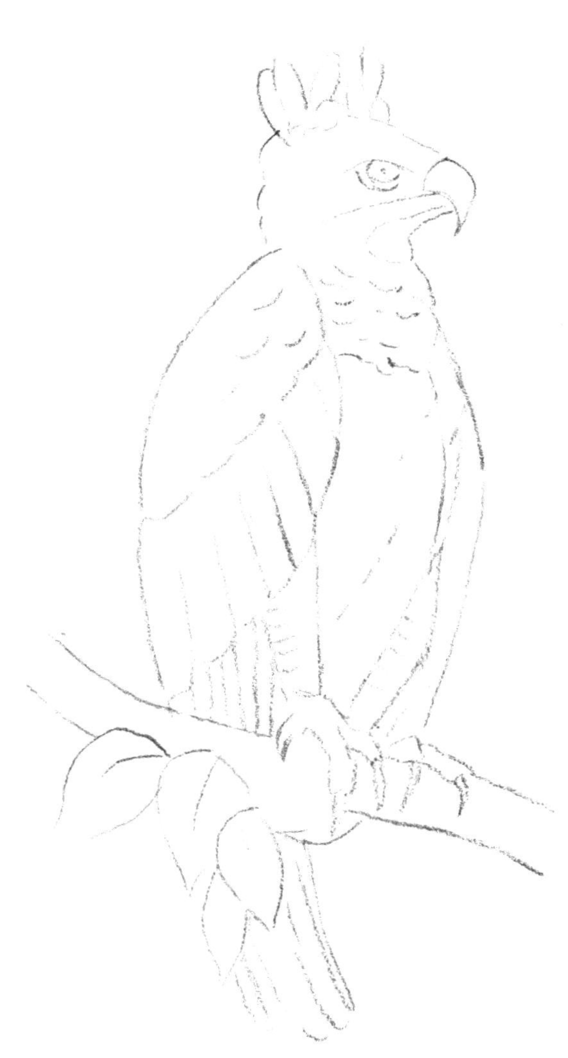

Mouse Deer

Also known as a chevrotain, this animal was once thought to have disappeared from the wild. It is about the size of a rabbit and is not a deer or a mouse at all, but rather the smallest hoofed animal in the world.

Using three colors and lots of dots, you'll create a little mouse deer of your own.

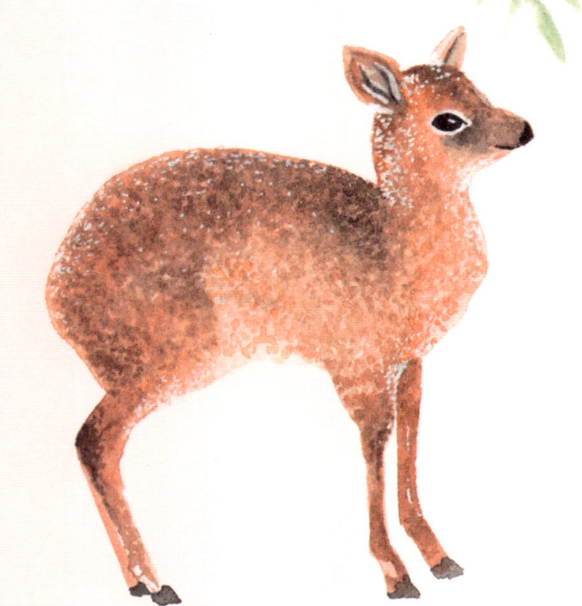

COLOR CHART

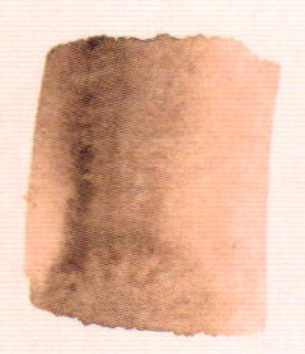

BURNT UMBER

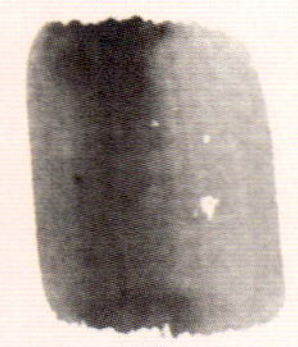

LAMP BLACK

YELLOW OCHRE

SUPPLIES

- Round brush (size 6 works well)
- 3 colors of paint
- Clean water
- Size 1 black ink pen
- White ink pen

1. Mix up a light, watery shade of Burnt Umber and apply it to the entire body of the animal. Let dry completely.
2. Using a slightly more concentrated mix of Burnt Umber, use the tip of your brush to dot on fur all over the body. Let dry.
3. Repeat the process again, darkening the Burnt Umber a little more as you go. Concentrate the darkest areas on the back of the mouse deer, the top of the head, muzzle and back leg. Paint the legs with a more solid effect.
4. Using a diluted shade of Lamp Black, add further dark dots to the shaded areas shown on the sample painting. Paint the hooves and darken the area around the corner of the eye.
5. Once dry, use your black ink pen to draw on the eyeball, nose, mouth and outlines in the ears.
6. With Yellow Ochre, add some dots randomly throughout the body fo- a sunlit effect.
7. With the white pen, add dots throughout the body, legs and head as highlights. Outline the eyeball and inside of the ears as well.

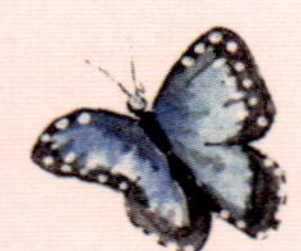

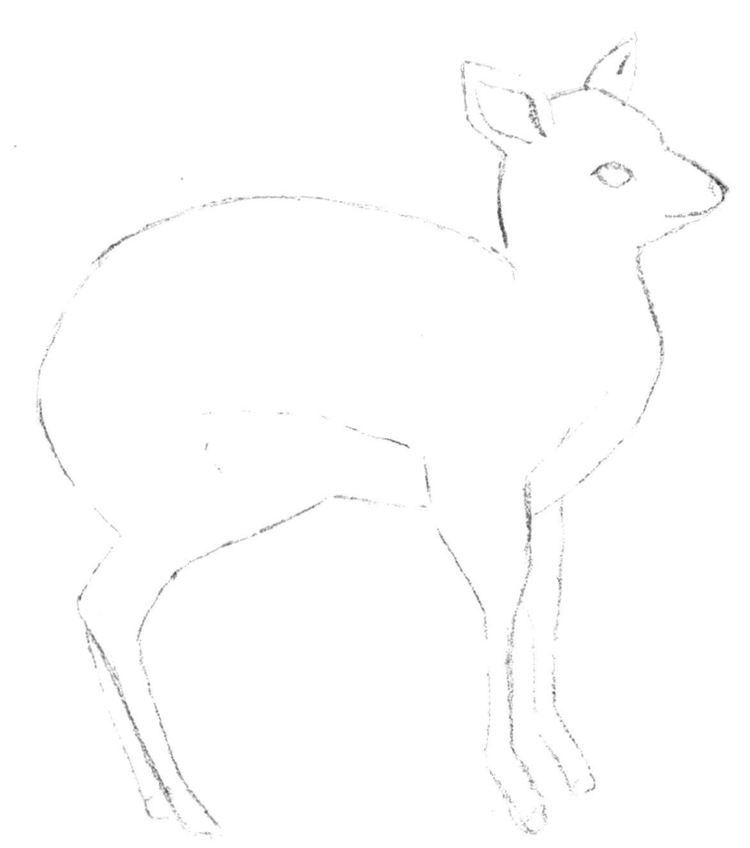

Pineapple

This sweet fruit is a staple in tropical locations! While only a couple of colors are used on both the top and bottom sections, the slight variances in tone will make each area stand out from the next, allowing your painting to be unique—just like a pineapple!

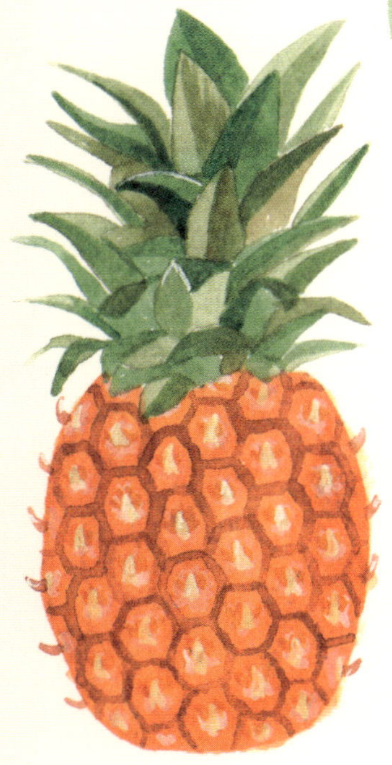

COLOR CHART

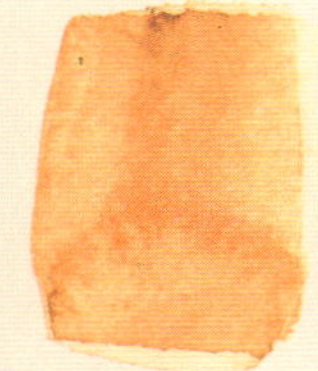

YELLOW OCHRE

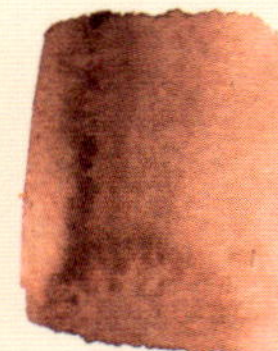

BURNT UMBER

SAP GREEN

HOOKER'S DARK GREEN

SUPPLIES

- Round brush (size 6 works well)
- 4 colors of paint
- Clean water
- Size 2 or smaller detail brush
- White ink pen

1. Start by filling in the base of the pineapple completely with Yellow Ochre and let it dry.
2. Using your smaller brush and Burnt Umber, create the outlines of the honeycomb shapes all over the base.
3. Moving onto the leaves, paint each one with Sap Green and let dry.
4. Using Hooker's Dark Green mixed with a little Burnt Umber, paint the tops and undersides of the leaves as shown in the sample image. This will help to separate each leaf and add dimension.
5. With your white ink pen, draw on the spikes on the body of the pineapple.
6. Using Burnt Umber, finish by adding curved spikes to the outside edges of the pineapple.

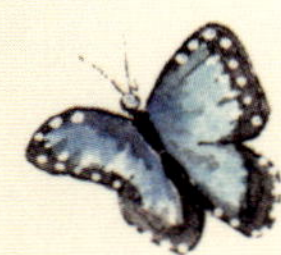

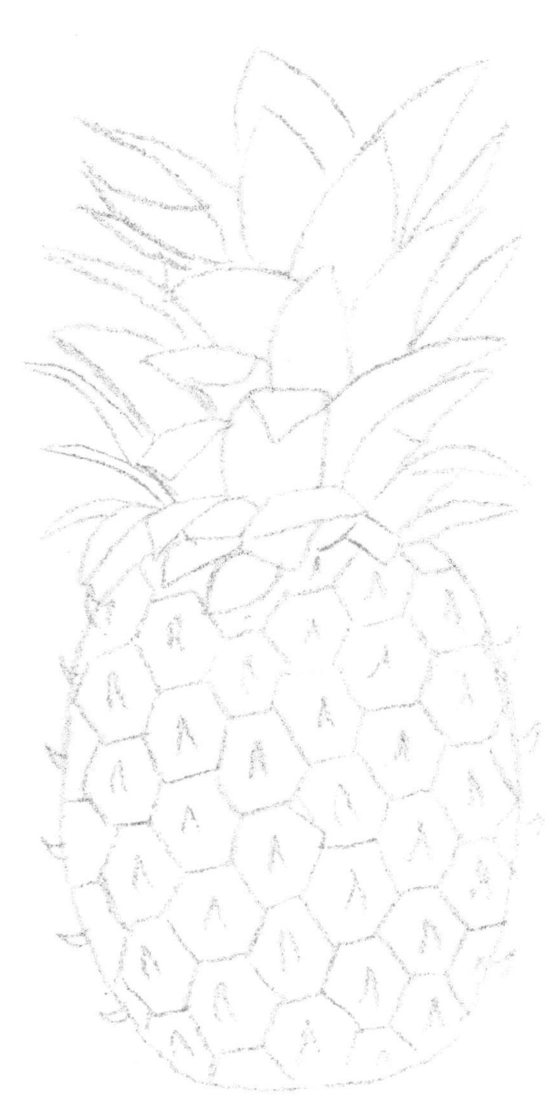

Tree Frog

This vibrant red-eyed tree frog is a staple in any jungle! Its colors are so beautiful but also serve a purpose! It is said that their bright bodies can over-stimulate predators and cause their eyes to see a ghost image of the frog as it jumps away.

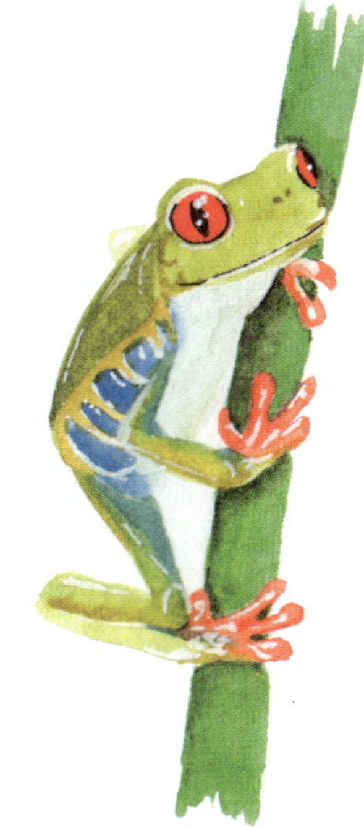

COLOR CHART

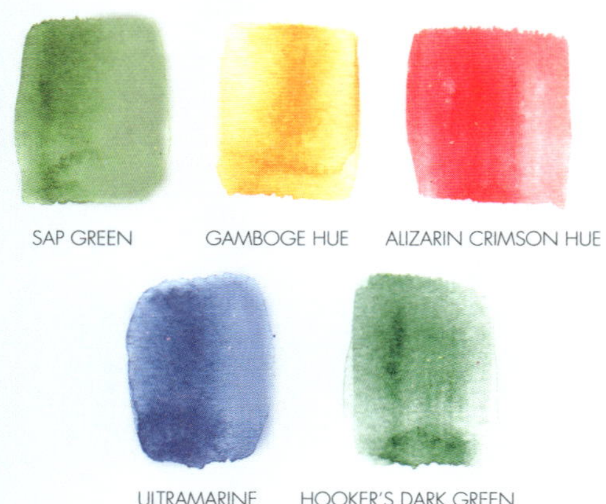

SUPPLIES

- Round brush (size 6 works well)
- 5 colors of paint
- Clean water
- Size 1 black ink pen
- White ink pen

1. Mix together Sap Green with a little bit of Gamboge Hue to create a more vibrant yellow-green. Start by applying this color to the face of the frog, followed by his back, arm and leg.
2. When that layer is dry, use Gamboge Hue to paint the lines on the belly area, and add a shadow to the leg fold.
3. Paint the eyeballs with a vibrant mixture of Alizarin Crimson Hue, then use a more diluted version to paint the fingers and toes of the frog.
4. Use Ultramarine to paint the stripe details on the belly and down the leg. Add a touch of the same color to the upper portion of the arm.
5. Mix together Sap Green with Hooker's Dark Green and paint the stem of the plant that the frog is holding onto. When dry, darken the areas under the body and arms of the frog with the same color to create a shadow effect.
6. Using your black ink pen, outline the eyeballs and fill in the pupils. Add the dots for the nostrils and lightly draw on the mouth.
7. Using your white ink pen, add highlights above the eyeballs, to the pupils, along the back of the frog, on the blue belly stripes, legs, fingers and toes.

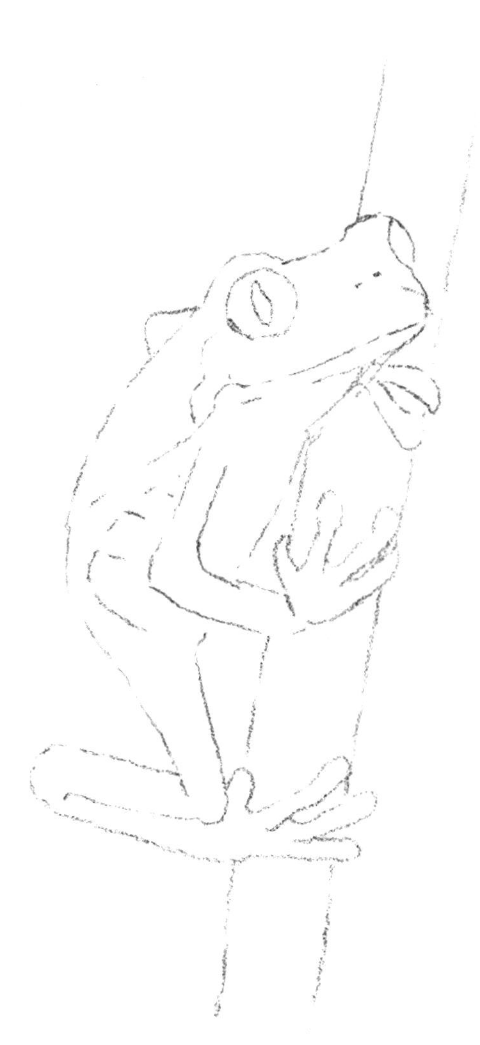

Bengal Tiger

This tiger lives in India and has the most gorgeous markings on its fur! The soft transition from orange to white topped with black stripes makes for a fun painting project.

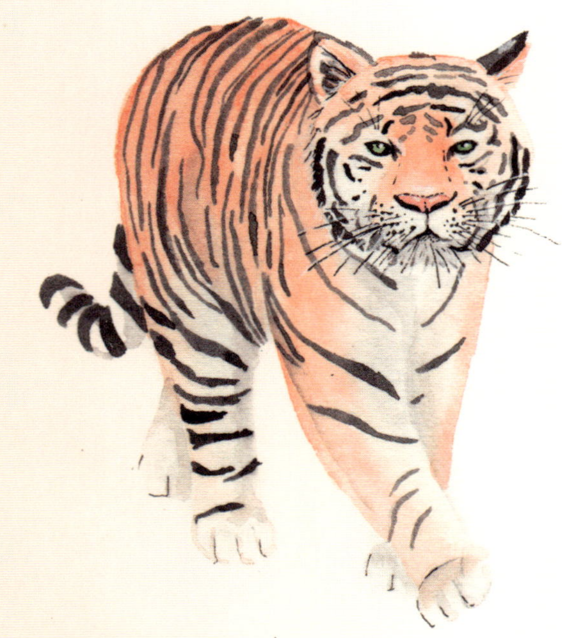

COLOR CHART

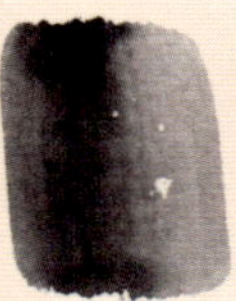
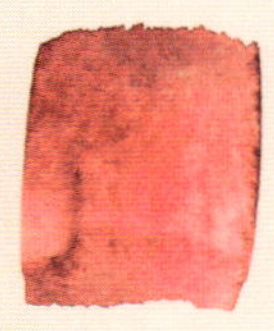

BURNT SIENNA   LAMP BLACK   INDIAN RED   SAP GREEN

SUPPLIES

- Round brush (size 6 works well)
- 4 colors of paint
- Clean water
- Size 2 or smaller detail brush
- Size 1 black ink pen
- White ink pen

1. Mix Burnt Sienna with water and apply it to the top body area of the tiger. Drag some of the color down the front legs and back leg. While the paint is still wet, clean off your brush and drag it along the edges of the orange shade to smooth and blend the color.

2. Apply the same shade to the top of the head, ears and down the nose. Once again, use your clean brush to smooth out any edges so there is a nice transition to the white.

3. Once dry, mix a little Lamp Black with water to create a very diluted light grey. Apply this color to the remaining white areas to make them stand out from the paper a little better.

4. Using your smaller brush, start painting on the stripes using Lamp Black. Paint the detail on the ears as well as the stripes on the head and face. You'll finish the finer details with the black pen in a minute!

5. With a very diluted shade of Indian Red, paint the nose. Then paint the eyes with Sap Green and let dry.

6. Use your black ink pen to draw the eyes, nose details, whiskers and facial details and to define the toes.

7. Use your white ink pen to add highlights to the eyes, nose and whiskers.

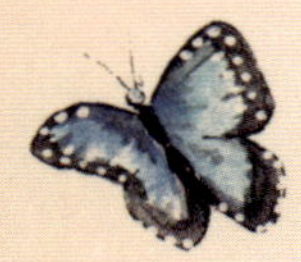

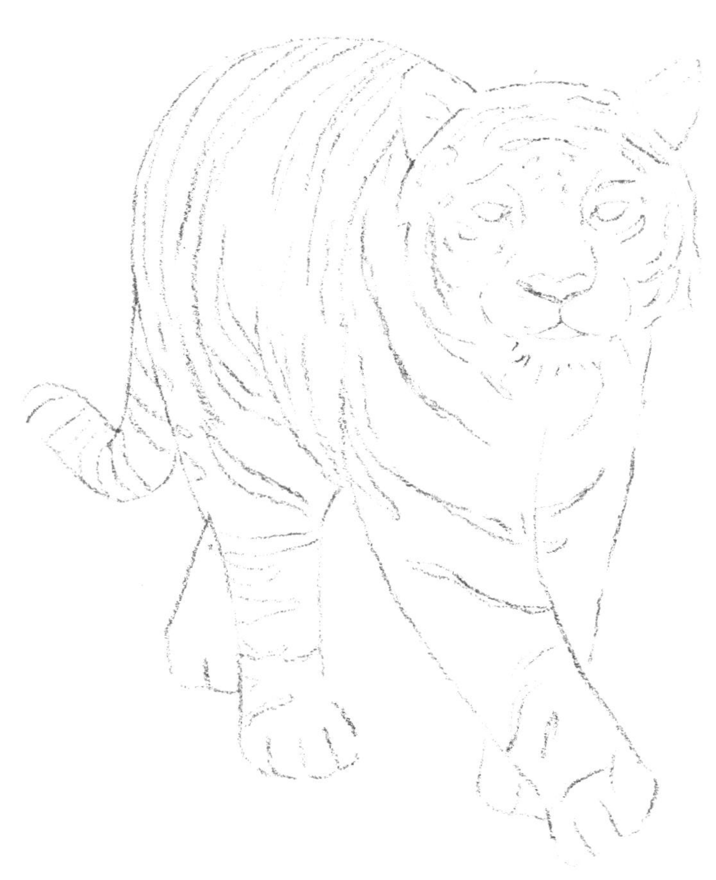

Squirrel Monkey

These adorable monkeys only measure about 12 inches (30.5 cm) long with a 16-inch (41-cm)-long tail! They spend their mornings looking for fruit and food to eat while bouncing around the trees. For this project, you'll focus on creating lots and lots of fur!

COLOR CHART

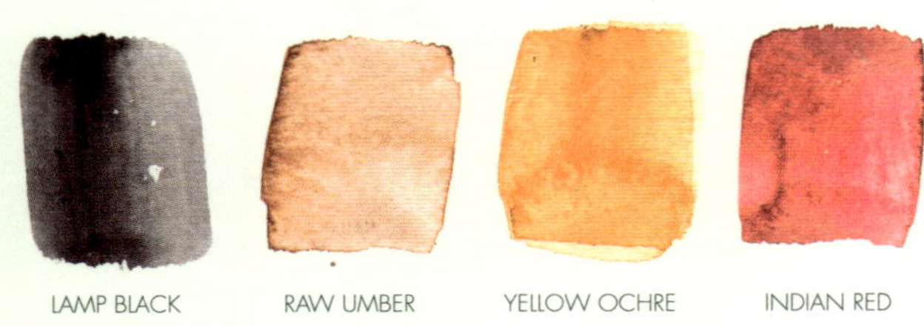

SUPPLIES

- Round brush (size 6 works well)
- 4 colors of paint
- Clean water
- Size 1 black ink pen
- White ink pen

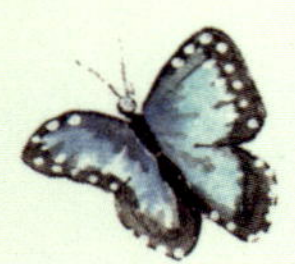

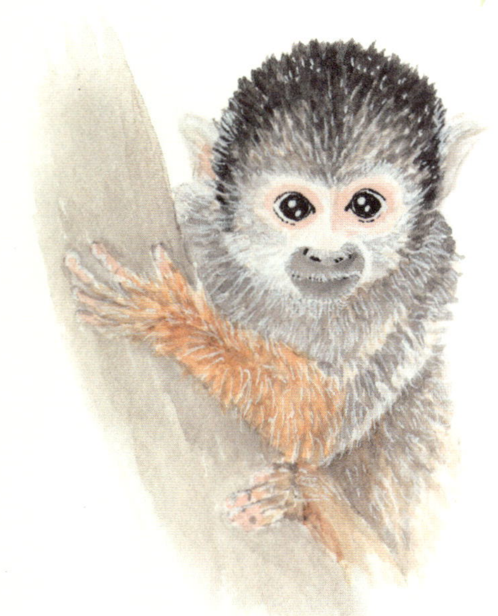

1. Starting with the top of the head, use the tip of your brush to create furry strokes with a medium shade of Lamp Black. As the paint dries, create another layer of a deeper Lamp Black along the top and sides of the head. Be sure to leave the eye area untouched.

2. Using that medium mix of Lamp Black again, start creating brush strokes of fur around the chest, arm and body of the monkey.

3. Once that layer is dry, create even more strokes using Raw Umber on the body and belly of the monkey. Add a few to the lighter area on the top of the head as well.

4. Using Yellow Ochre, create furry brush strokes on the arm and foot. Add in some Raw Umber strokes when the yellow has dried.

5. Dilute Indian Red to create a pink shade. Paint the face around the eyes with this shade, as well as the fingers, toes and center of the ears.

6. Paint the grey muzzle around the nose with a medium shade of Lamp Black, then paint the tree trunk with a mix of diluted Raw Umber and Lamp Black. Darken the areas around the arms with more Lamp Black and define the fingers.

7. Use your black pen to draw on the eyes, nose details and mouth. Using the white ink pen, highlight the eyes and create small, short strokes all over the monkey to highlight the fur and make the piece come together.

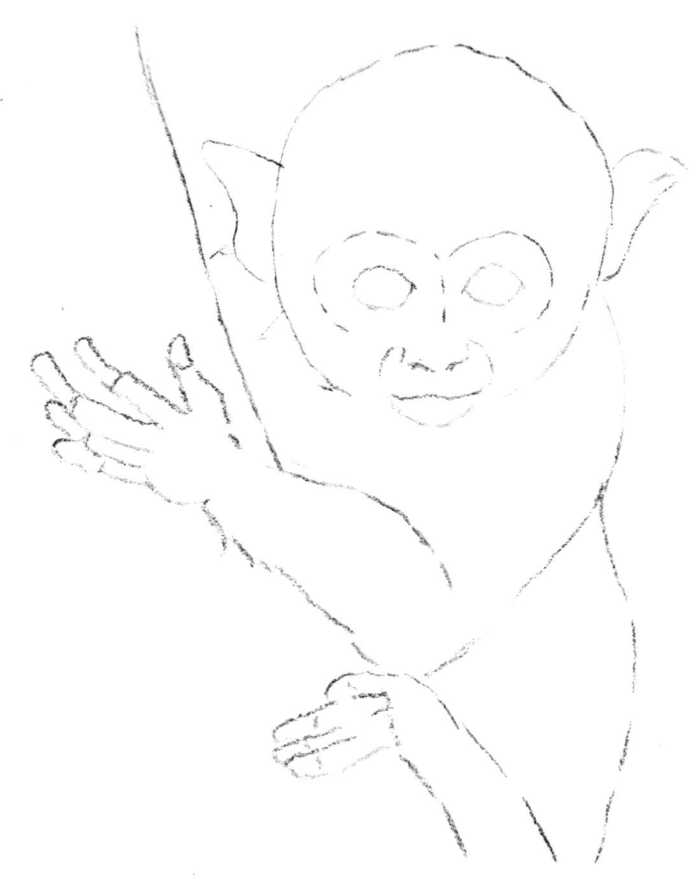

Poison Dart Frog

These frogs come in so many vibrant color combinations, like this bright blue version. Don't get too close though! These guys contain enough venom under their skin to do some serious damage.

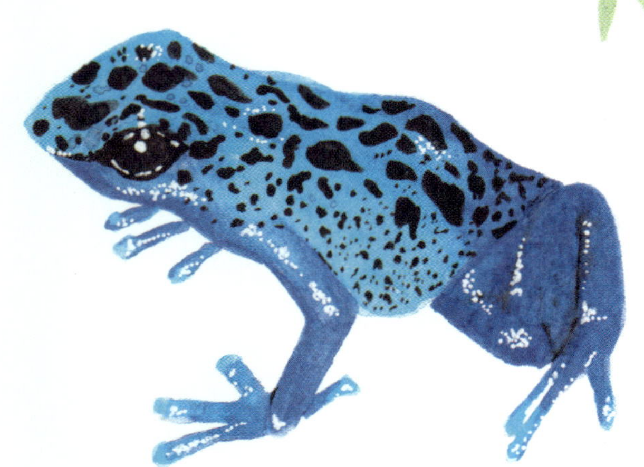

COLOR CHART

CERULEAN BLUE HUE

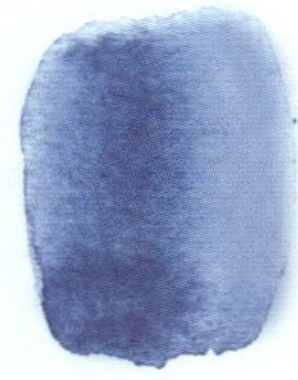

ULTRAMARINE

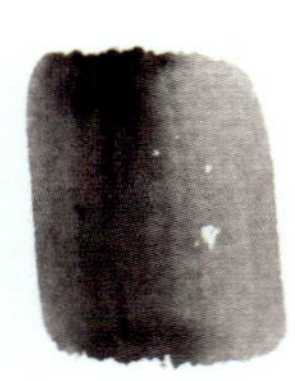

LAMP BLACK

SUPPLIES

- Round brush (size 6 works well)
- 3 colors of paint
- Clean water
- Size 2 or smaller detail brush
- White ink pen

1. Mix Cerulean Blue Hue with some water and apply to the entire body of the frog, excluding the eyeball. Let this layer dry completely.
2. For the second layer, mix a more concentrated pigment of Ultramarine and apply it to the front arm, starting at the wrist and moving upwarc. As you get to the elbow, rinse and wipe off your brush. Use the dryer brush to help fade the color into the body and under the chin. You may have to rinse, wipe and blend multiple times.
3. Use this same technique on the bum of the frog, blending Ultramarine into his back.
4. Paint a solid layer of Ultramarine over the back leg, using the clean, wipe and blend technique as you get to the toes. Finish the remaining hands in the same way.
5. Once the piece is completely dry, use your smaller brush to start adding Lamp Black spots to the head and back of the frog. Make these blobby shapes up as you go! Some larger, some smaller. The dots should be smaller on the belly portion.
6. Fill in the eyeball with Lamp Black as well and let it dry. Add the crecses on the back leg too.
7. Use your white ink pen to add the highlight spot in the eyeball and tc indicate the rim of the eye with a few short, tiny strokes around the edge. Stipple on some highlights to the arms, legs, fingers and back to make this frog look glossy!

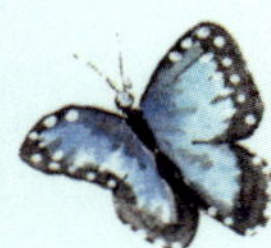

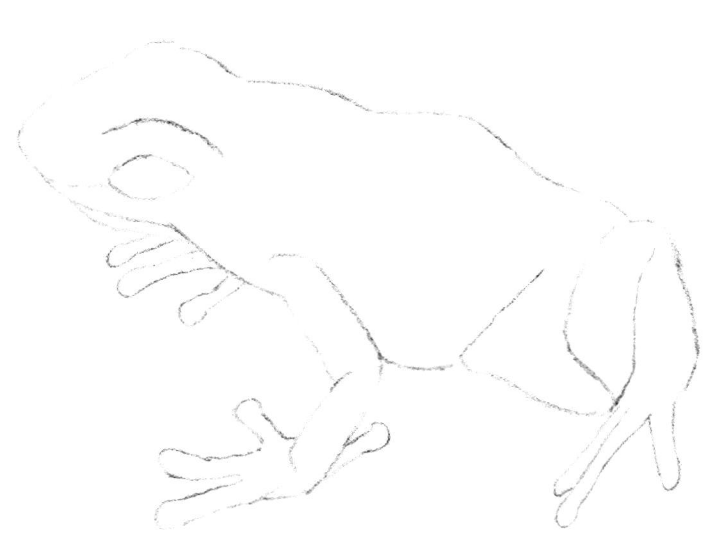

Slow Loris

These adorable creatures are one of the rarest of the primates and have huge eyes that can see in the dark.

You'll only need three colors to complete this project and will fade the shades from dark to light using a wipe-and-blend technique.

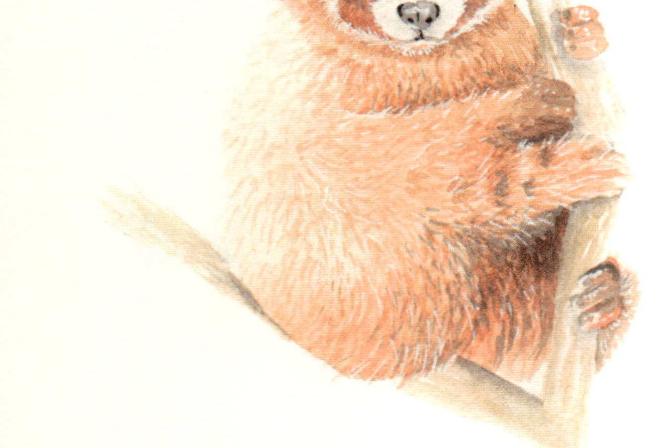

COLOR CHART

RAW UMBER

BURNT UMBER

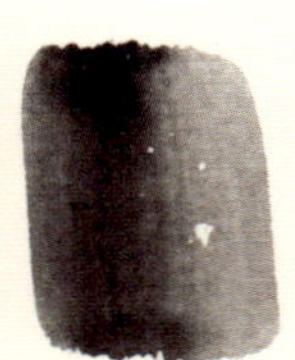

LAMP BLACK

SUPPLIES

- Round brush (size 6 works well)
- 3 colors of paint
- Clean water
- Size 2 or smaller detail brush
- Size 1 black ink pen
- White ink pen

1. Apply a wash of Raw Umber to the right-hand side of the body. Before the layer dries completely, rinse off your brush, wipe it, then use it to blend the edge out to a lighter shade on the left. Continue blending like this until you're happy with the gradient.

2. When dry, use Burnt Umber to add darker shadows above the top arm, around the chin and the inside of the leg. Use the rinse, wipe and blend technique to fade out the edges. Let dry completely.

3. Using your smaller brush and Raw Umber, create fur strokes following the direction of the body. Make these strokes lighter toward the left-hand side of the body. Let dry.

4. Add another layer of fur strokes using Burnt Umber and concentrating them on the right-hand side where the fur is darker. To darken areas even more, use a small amount of Lamp Black. Continue building the fur layers until you are happy with the light-to-dark appearance. Add definition to the hands and feet using Lamp Black.

5. Paint the mask on the face and the ears with Burnt Umber and let dry. Using a light mix of Raw Umber, create small strokes throughout the white areas.

6. Paint the nose using a light mix of Lamp Black and the eyes with Burnt Umber. Paint the tree branch with a mix of Raw Umber and Lamp Black, adding more Lamp Black around the body for shadow detailing.

7. Using your black ink pen, outline the eyes and draw the pupils, mouth and nostril details. Use the white pen to add highlights around the eyes, inside the iris and throughout the body using fur strokes.

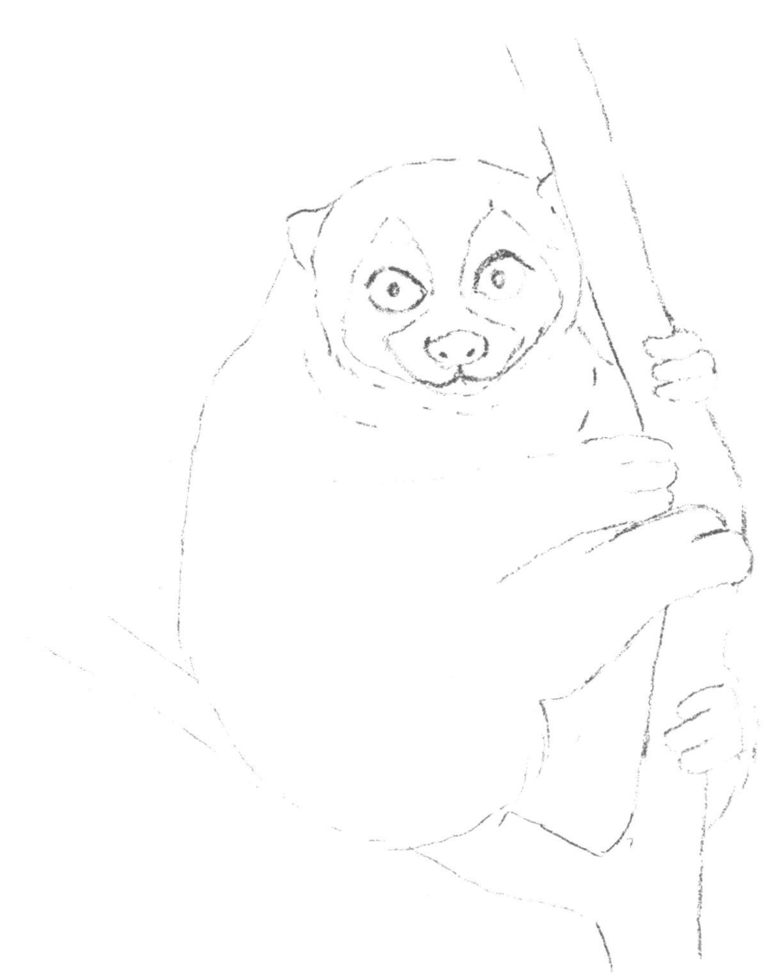

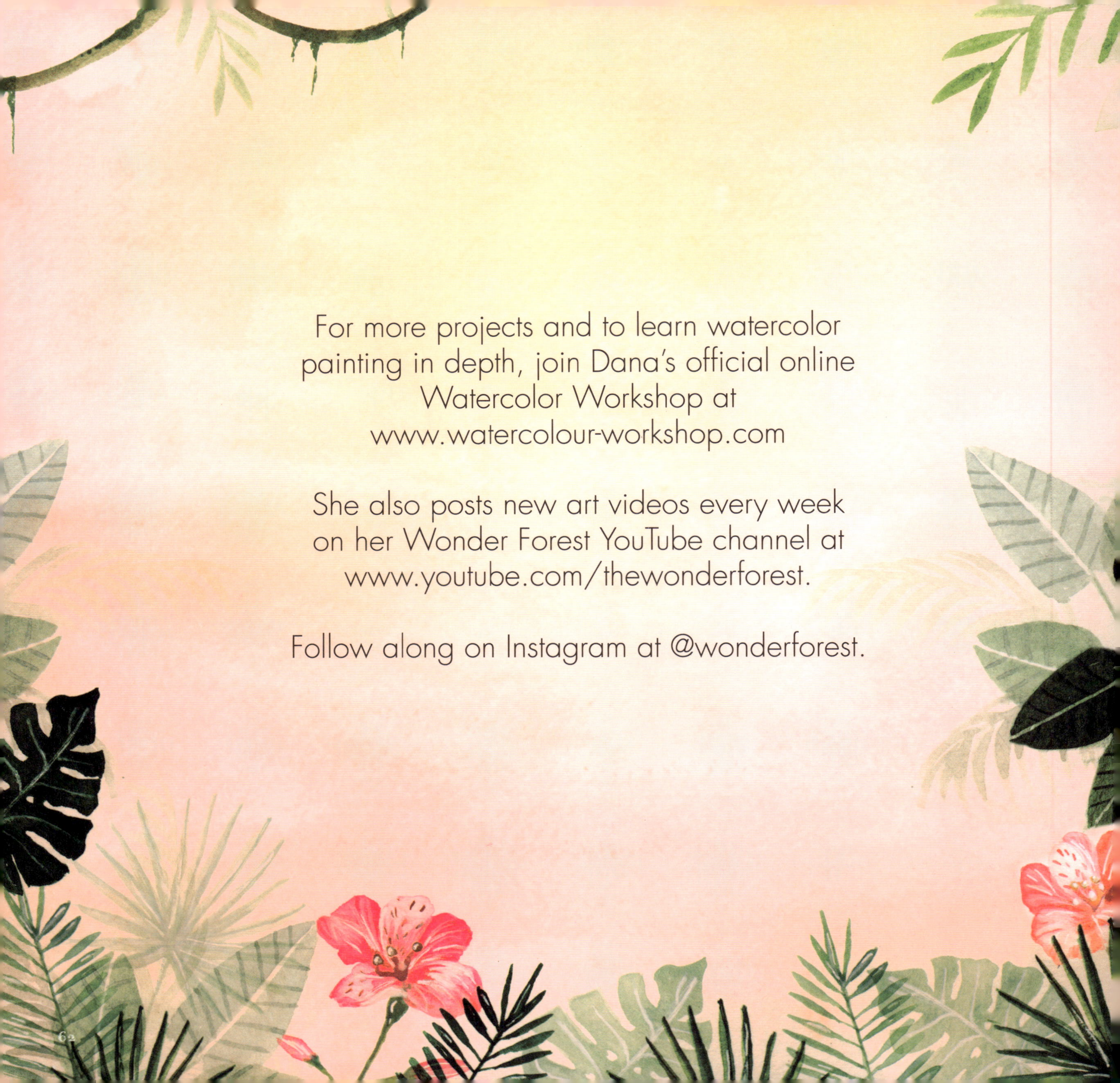

For more projects and to learn watercolor painting in depth, join Dana's official online Watercolor Workshop at www.watercolour-workshop.com

She also posts new art videos every week on her Wonder Forest YouTube channel at www.youtube.com/thewonderforest.

Follow along on Instagram at @wonderforest.

ABOUT THE AUTHOR

Dana is a Canada-based artist, founder of the Wonder Forest® product brand and owner of Dana Fox Creative, a small art and design studio.

Although she has a lifetime of traditional art training, she spent over a decade building her career as a website and digital designer before rediscovering painting as a method of relaxation and anxiety management.

"I fell in love with watercolor and how calming the practice was. I was able to eliminate stress and express my feelings through art, unlike I had before."

With her extensive background in technical digital work, she began creating patterns and watercolor designs for home decor items and tech accessories, which can be found in stores worldwide including Bloomingdale's, Target, Nordstrom, Wayfair and Urban Outfitters.

Dana has since started teaching watercolor painting online and is the author of the Watercolor with Me book series.

INDEX